They Shall See His Face

Studies in Chinese Christianity

G. Wright Doyle and Carol Lee Hamrin,
Series Editors

A Project of the Global China Center

www.globalchinacenter.org

Previously published volumes in the series

Carol Lee Hamrin & Stacey Bieler, eds., *Salt and Light: Lives of Faith That Shaped Modern China*, volume 1

Carol Lee Hamrin & Stacey Bieler, eds., *Salt and Light: More Lives of Faith That Shaped Modern China*, volume 2

Richard R. Cook & David W. Pao, eds., *After Imperialism: Christian Identity in China and the Global Evangelical Movement*

Carol Lee Hamrin & Stacey Bieler, *Salt and Light: More Lives of Faith That Shaped Modern China*, volume 3

Lit-sen Chang, *Wise Man from the East: Lit-sen Chang (Zhang Lisheng)*

George Hunter McNeur, *Liang A-Fa: China's First Preacher, 1789–1855*

Eunice V. Johnson, *Timothy Richard's Vision: Education and Reform in China, 1880–1910*

G. Wright Doyle, *Builders of the Chinese Church: Pioneer Protestant Missionaries and Chinese Church Leaders*

Jack R. Lundbom, *On the Road to Siangyang: Covenant Mission in Mainland China 1890–1949*

Brent Fulton, *China's Urban Christians: A Light That Cannot Be Hidden*

Andrew T. Kaiser, *The Rushing on of the Purposes of God: Christian Missions in Shanxi since 1876*

Li Ma & Jin Li, *Surviving the State, Remaking the Church: A Sociological Portrait of Christians in Mainland China*

Linda Banks and Robert Banks, *Through the Valley of the Shadow: Australian Women in War-Torn China*

Arthur Lin, *The History of Christian Missions in Guangxi, China*

Linda Banks and Robert Banks, *They Shall See His Face: The Story of Amy Oxley Wilkinson and Her Visionary Work among the Blind in China*

"In *They Shall See His Face*, Linda and Robert Banks have rescued an important and fascinating story from the gathering mists of history and made it available to the larger public. Their careful detective work (as they call it) has given us a story of God's grace in people's lives that both inspires and instructs."

—HOWARD A. SNYDER
Author of *The Problem of Wineskins* and *Models of the Kingdom*

"These days it is not unusual to run into a church or choir composed of blind people in major Chinese cities. But few could imagine the immense hardship Amy Oxley Wilkinson braved at the turn of the twentieth century in bringing education to the visually impaired in a pragmatic society where disability was conveniently sidelined. This amazing story illustrates how the gospel of Jesus may be perched not only through words but also through deeds, especially works among the disadvantaged."

—WINGYAN MOKCHAN
Visiting Professor, China Graduate School of Theology, Hong Kong

"This book tells the story of a courageous and passionate missionary and her legacy among the blind in China. The authors' great achievement is to do this in a way that their own voice seems to disappear and that of Amy Oxley Wilkinson shines through. It is a historical biography grounded in impeccable research, providing insight into the contribution (and colonial prejudices) of Christian mission to social justice at the turn of the twentieth century. The prose is beautiful and photographs delightful. The book deserves a wide audience."

—SHANE CLIFTON
Author of *Crippled Grace: Disability, Virtue Ethics, and the Good Life*

"Linda and Robert Banks' fascinating account presents Amy Oxley Wilkinson's life in its vibrant historical, cultural, and political contexts. This is missionary biography at its best: rich, real, and relevant. The world needs to hear this story of heroism, Christian conviction, and love for the Chinese people. Everyone should be challenged to do good specifically where God and their conscience direct. Highly recommended!"

—WEI-HAN KUAN
State Director, Church Missionary Society, Victoria, Australia

"Amy Oxley Wilkinson proves that a young Australian woman can leave a lasting legacy for the poor and disabled. She followed God's leading at a dangerous time in a foreign culture to meet the needs of children without help and hope. This is a truly inspiring real-life story worth reading and retelling."

—RUSSELL CLARK
Former Head of the Department of Medicine, United Christian Hospital, Kowloon, Hong Kong; and Kay Clark, CMS Missionaries, Hong Kong

"A most uplifting story of Amy Oxley Wilkinson and her amazing ministry at the Blind School in Foochow. One cannot help but be inspired by her life of commitment to mission in China and ministry of love and care. Read this book to be challenged in your faith and renewed in your commitment to the Lord."

—KUA WEE SENG
Director, United Bible Societies, China Partnership, Singapore

"*They Shall See His Face* is a beautifully written piece on the faith and passion of Amy Oxley Wilkinson. The love that she had for children in China with low vision and blindness is captured perfectly in this historically detailed book. She valued them simply as children, not as children with disabilities. Her compelling story is a guide to anyone working within the health industry and education."

—LAUREN ROUSE
Occupational Therapist and Braille Transcriber, The Statewide Vision Resource Centre, Melbourne, Australia

They Shall See His Face

Amy Oxley Wilkinson and Her Visionary Education
of the Blind in China

LINDA AND ROBERT BANKS

☙PICKWICK *Publications* • Eugene, Oregon

THEY SHALL SEE HIS FACE
Amy Oxley Wilkinson and Her Visionary Education of the Blind in China
Studies in Chinese Christianity

Copyright © 2021 Linda Banks and Robert Banks. All rights reserved. Except for brief quotations in critical publications or reviews, no part of this book may be reproduced in any manner without prior written permission from the publisher. Write: Permissions, Wipf and Stock Publishers, 199 W. 8th Ave., Suite 3, Eugene, OR 97401.

Pickwick Publications
An Imprint of Wipf and Stock Publishers
199 W. 8th Ave., Suite 3
Eugene, OR 97401

www.wipfandstock.com

PAPERBACK ISBN: 978-1-7252-6033-7
HARDCOVER ISBN: 978-1-7252-8413-5
EBOOK ISBN: 978-1-7252-8414-2

Cataloguing-in-Publication data:

Names: Banks, Linda, author. | Banks, Robert, 1939–, author.

Title: They shall see his face : Amy Oxley Wilkinson and her visionary education of the blind in China / Linda Banks and Robert Banks.

Description: Eugene, OR: Pickwick Publications, 2021. | Studies in Chinese Christianity. | Includes bibliographical references.

Identifiers: ISBN 978-1-7252-6033-7 (paperback). | ISBN 978-1-7252-8413-5 (hardcover). | ISBN 978-1-7252-8414-2 (ebook).

Subjects: LCSH: Missions—China—History. | Missionaries—China—Biography. | Women missionaries—Biography.

Classification: BV3427 A1 B355 2021 (paperback). | BV3427 (ebook).

02/23/21

Scripture quotations are taken from the Holy Bible, New International Version®, NIV® Copyright © 1973, 1978, 1984, 2011 by Biblica, Inc.® Used by permission. All rights reserved worldwide.

Original version published by Acorn Press
An imprint of Bible Society Australia
ACN 148 058 306
GPO Box 9874
Sydney NSW 2001
Australia
© 2017 Linda and Robert Banks

To our good friend Andrew Lu,
without whose vision and generosity
this book may never have been written

Contents

Sources of Images | ix
List of Images | xi
References to Places | xiii
Acknowledgments | xv
Prologue | xix

1 Signals of China Calling (1868–1895) | 1
2 The Blind Boy in the Ditch (1896–1900) | 14
3 Surprises of the Heart (1901–1906) | 35
4 A Travelling Sight and Sound Show (1907–1914) | 53
5 The Order of the Golden Grain (1915–1920) | 72
6 From the Far East to the East End (1921–1949) | 90

Afterword | 110
Bibliography | 115

Sources of Images

The authors wish to thank the following individuals and organisations for permission to reproduce their material in this book:

A. & E. Hope Family Collection—04, 06, 19, 20, 21.

Hazelton Private Collection—11, 18, 25, 26, 29, 31, 34.

Robert and Linda Banks Family Collection—02, 03, 09, 12, 15, 16, 24, 28, 32, 35.

Church Missionary Society Australia Archives—01, 05, 10, 30.

Church Missionary Society Britain Archives—17, 22.

Emmanuel College Cambridge Archives—13.

David M. Rubenstein Rare Book and Manuscript Library, Duke University—23.

Harvard-Yenching Library, Harvard College Library, Harvard University—14.

The remaining images—03, 08, 33 are in the public domain.

List of Images

01 Amy Oxley, aged 25. Courtesy of the Church Missionary Society Australia Archives | xvii

02 The main branches of Amy Oxley's family tree | 2

03 St Paul's Cobbitty | 3

04 Nurse Amy at Sydney Hospital for Sick Children | 7

05 Robert Stewart, in a photo taken by Amy at "Darriwill." | 10

06 The Marsden Training Home, with Eliza (sitting, left) and Amy (standing, left), c. 1893. | 10

07 Kucheng martyrs' graves on Nantai Island, Foochow | 13

08 Old City of Foochow, looking up towards Kuliang | 16

09 Map of central Fukien Province | 18

10 Amy in dinghy alongside *The Messenger of Peace* | 20

11 Handwritten letter to Isabel, 16 November 1898 | 28

12 Amy, Minna (left), Sophie (middle), and Bible Class at Deng Doi | 29

13 Early students at the Blind Boys School | 32

15 George Wilkinson (2nd row, 2nd from right) at Cambridge | 39

15 The Soul-Lighted School with Bible motto above entrance | 40

16 St John's Church, Nantai, where Amy and George married | 44

17 Students on exercise equipment | 47

18 Older student serving in Hospital | 47

19 The Blind School and Hospital, c. 1905 | 50

20 Amy, George and Isabel relaxing at "Darriwill," 1908 | 54

List of Images

21 George Wilkinson, working from home in the hospital compound c. 1909 | 59

22 Amy and Band on tour, c. 1909 | 64

23 Amy teaching balance on exercise equipment | 68

24 Boys at the Blind School matting and weaving | 68

25 Amy and George, with Marsden and Isabel, in London, 1915 | 73

26 Postcard from Isabel to her father, pre-addressed by George | 75

27 Red Cross drill at the school | 80

28 The travelling Blind Boys Band | 81

29 Amy's Order of the Golden Grain Medal | 87

30 CMS Exhibition in the Agricultural Hall, London, 1922 | 92

31 Amy being presented to Queen Mary at the CMS Exhibition, 1922 | 94

32 The Blind Boys Band that toured England, 1922 | 96

33 Chinese in Limehouse during the 1930 | 102

34 Amy, wearing her Order of the Golden Grain and Viceroy's Medals, c. 1930 | 105

35 Amy and George's graves in Tunbridge Wells | 112

References to Places

To preserve the historical atmosphere and avoid confusion when reading quotes from primary sources, the older spelling of place names in China has been retained:

Amoy (Xiamen)

Canton (Guangzhou)

Deng Doi (Dongdai)

Foochow (Fuzhou)

Fukien (Fujian)

Kucheng (Gutian)

Kuliang (Guling)

Lieng Kong (Liangjiang)

Nanking (Nanjing)

Ningpo (Ningbo)

Peking (Beijing)

Swatow (Shantou)

Tientsin (Tianjin)

In addition, imperial rather than metric distance measurements have been used in the main text to correspond with quotations from the time. The Chinese characters for 'The Soul-Lighted School', 靈光盲學校, have been used to mark section breaks.

Acknowledgments

RESEARCH AND WRITING A book is a lot like being a detective. It involves accessing various kinds of information, only some available in print, and is dependent on the contribution of many different people. The research, mainly undertaken by Linda, took us to five countries, some more than once, over the best part of a decade, and the writing was done in three different places over a further year.

We would like to acknowledge the following people for providing vital material. Amy's maternal Australian relatives, Ellen and Alistair Hope, preserved and painstakingly transcribed a collection of family letters and diaries covering the beginning of Amy's time in China. Amy's English grandson Peter Hazelton and his daughter Ruth Horne helped us in details of her post-China years. Ruth has been a vital conversation partner in the writing of the book.

Key documents relating to Amy's work in China were found in the excellent resources of the Australian National University, especially from the work of Dr. Ian Welch; the Church Missionary Society Australia Archives in Sydney; the National Library of Australia in Canberra; Trinity Theological College in Singapore; Hong Kong Baptist University; the Crowther Mission Studies Library in Oxford; the Church Missionary Society Archives through Adam Matthew Digital; Edward Cadbury Centre at the University of Birmingham, for the Hazelton Family Collection; Fujian Normal University Library, for some historical sources; and Moore Theological College Library, for recordings by Deaconess Mary Andrews about and by the Fuzhou Blind School Choir.

We are also indebted to George Niu, who gave us valuable help on Chinese idioms, customs, and early missionary history; Australian cultural historian Professor David Walker, for his general encouragement and knowledge of early Australia–China political relations; Lauren Rouse of the

Royal Society of the Blind, Canberra; and John Burge, local historian at St Paul's Church, Cobbitty.

Chinese friends who showed us aspects of Amy's life and world in Fujian Province include Professor Chen Zhaofen and Pastors Chen Lifu, Yu Israel, and Kuo Enoch of the historic Flower Lane Church in Fuzhou. The principal, past principal, staff, and alumnae of Fuzhou Blind School gave us access to important artifacts and photos, as well as the opportunity to take part in their International White Cane Day celebration. Thanks also to Brian Horne for his video recording of this event; to Dr. Zhang Jihong, our translator for the discussion afterwards; and to Chen Jun'en and Pan Liying Puyang, the author and translator of the short history of the School.

We are deeply grateful for the personal encouragement and financial support arranged by Dr. Wei-Han Kuan, State Director of the Church Missionary Society Victoria, through the Keith Cole Publishing Fund, and once again to Mr Andrew Lu for his continuing interest and financial generosity.

We appreciated working with our friend Greg Clarke, then CEO of the Bible Society Australia, and with Kris Argall, Acorn Press' deputy editor, on the original version of this book, and with G. Wright Doyle of the Global China Center, and K. C. Hanson of Wipf and Stock Publishers, on its revision for an international audience. The only substantial change we have made to the original text is to compress the Australian material on Amy Oxley Wilkinson's family and religious background.

Linda and Robert Banks
July 2020

Amy Oxley, aged 25. Courtesy of the Church Missionary Society Australia Archives

Prologue

It was Christmas Eve 1980, not long after China reopened to the West.

A man, whose family had emigrated from southeast China shortly before the communist revolution, had just returned to Fuzhou, the capital of Fujian Province. After dining in a downtown restaurant, he started to walk home. It was cold and wet that night, with a wind blowing down from the surrounding mountains.

As he wandered through the historic Three Lanes and Seven Alleys area, the man looked for any reminders of his childhood. Glancing at buildings he used to pass, including where a large church once stood, little remained of an earlier time.

"How sad," he said to himself. As he walked on, he heard an unusual sound carried by the winter wind. Someone further down the street was playing the flute to a tune he knew well:

> Joy to the world! The Lord is come.
> Let earth receive her King!

As he approached, in the half-light he could just make out an aged, blind beggar dressed in rags. He recognised the man's face immediately.

"Excuse me," he said in local dialect. "I am the son of Pastor Ding, who used to be well known in this area. You might not know me, but surely you remember my late father?"

The old man lowered his flute, looked bewildered for a moment, then shook his head decisively. "No, sir. I am a humble beggar, blind and useless throughout my life. I am the refuse of this socialist state and a burden to the people. I swear that I don't know of any pastor or foreigner. I am sorry."

"But how can this be?" the other man said. "I remember you. I heard you playing and singing in the Blind Boys Band when I was a child. Weren't you one of Mrs Amy Wilkinson's students? In fact, one of the nine who travelled with her to England?"

Starting to utter something, the blind man suddenly fell silent. The deep furrows on his face and bent frame told of the hardships he had endured over the years.

Overcome by a flash of inspiration, the pastor's son started to sing tentatively in English,

Amazing grace, how sweet the sound
that saved a wretch like me.
I once was lost, but now am found . . .

The old man unexpectedly began to cry and through his tears joined in the song—open faced, sounding like a young man, and with the voice of an angel.

. . . Was blind, but now I see!

The two embraced each other as one and held each other for a long time into the night.[1]

---

1. This story was related to the authors by George Ngu, a local Chinese historian.

1

Signals of China Calling
(1868–1895)

THE EARLY EVENING OF Monday 13 January 1868 was still hot and humid in Camden, as the seventh child of John and Harriet Oxley (nee Hassall) was born at "Kirkham." Amy Isabel Oxley's first years were spent in this family home, approximately thirty miles southwest of Sydney, described as "the most valuable country estate in the County."[1] Built in 1816 by her paternal grandparents, John and Emma Oxley, "Kirkham" was a large stately home with ten generous bedrooms for family and guests. Its spacious loft was the place where her maternal great grandfather, Rev Samuel Marsden, held the first church service in the district. "Kirkham" was hedged around by beautifully sculpted gardens, with a variety of European trees and shrubs. This large farming property included several other substantial workers' cottages, a state-of-the-art steam flour mill, double-storied stables, a productive dairy, and a boutique vineyard that produced fine wine for export. As well as supervising the running of the property, Amy's father, John Norton Oxley, served as a magistrate and represented the district in New South Wales' first Parliament.[2] Her mother, Harriet, organized the domestic duties and children's education, especially as her husband was often away on business.[3]

---

1. *Sydney Morning Herald*, 3 December 1870.

2. Additional information on John Norton Oxley may be found in the *Dictionary of Sydney*, 2008, accessed June 2015.

3. The following details come from correspondence between Harriet and her cousin Marianne Hope, held by her descendants in the Hope Family Collection.

Amy's parents lived on nearby farms in the area. Her father was the son of a famous explorer, John Oxley, and her mother the granddaughter of a pioneer clergyman, Samuel Marsden. Harriet's father, Rev Thomas Hassall, a child of missionaries to the South Sea Islands, had originally been Samuel's assistant and married his daughter Anne. He had also founded the first Sunday School in the colony and, because his parish covered so much territory, was known as the "galloping parson."[4] John Norton and Harriet both attended nearby St Paul's church in Cobbitty, the main church in the parish, and were married there by Thomas in February 1854.

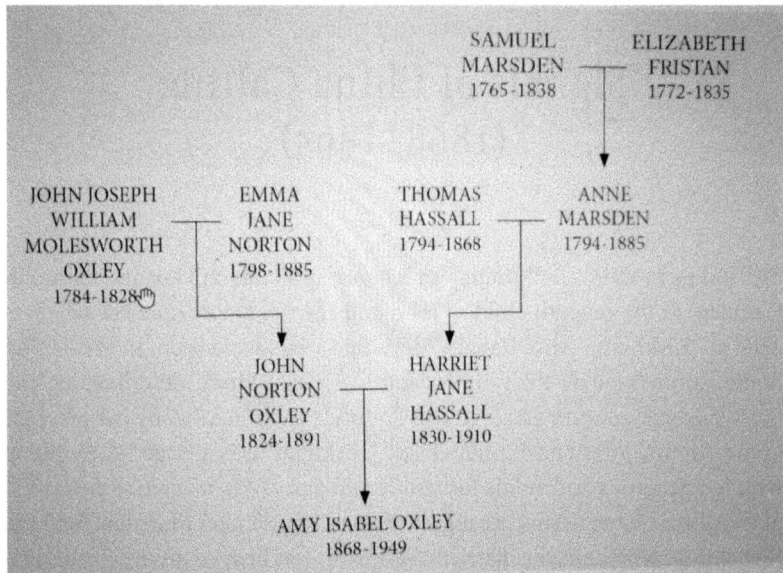

02 The main branches of Amy Oxley's family tree

Life at "Kirkham" largely reflected upper middle-class Victorian values and routines. A live-in tutor taught the school-age children the basic subjects connected to "reading, writing, and arithmetic," history and geography. Activities like swimming, riding, and shooting, as well as calisthenics, rounded out the curriculum. Popular children's games of the period—such as skipping, jacks, and marbles, Oranges and Lemons, and What's the Time, Mr Wolf?—were all considered worthwhile educational play. Amy's sisters learned the piano and singing. Duets were a favorite pastime for friends and visitors, and occasionally their mother accompanied them on the harmonium. By making doll's clothes, they were also taught to darn, sew, and knit.

4. See Reeson, "Thomas Hassall," in *ADEB*, 159–60 and Hassall, In Old Australia, 1902.

A girl learned "a skill with her needle and the art of cutting out, which will be valuable in her future years."⁵

Routines at "Kirkham" sought to naturally integrate the Christian faith into the children's lives. Morning and evening prayers, as well as Bible reading, were part of their everyday experience. Involvement in the life of St Paul's Cobbitty, their local church, was a highlight of the week. This was often followed by extended family gatherings at nearby "Denbigh," home of her late grandfather, Thomas Hassall, and his wife Anne Marsden, matriarch of the whole clan. Sunday lunch was full of engrossing stories about the lives and exploits of her distinguished forbears, sometimes illustrated by artifacts and pictures displayed on the walls of the house.

03 St Paul's Cobbitty

It was here that Amy first began to learn about how her great grandfather Samuel Marsden, the son of a Yorkshire blacksmith, was financially supported by the social reformer William Wilberforce to study for the ministry at Cambridge University; became the first assistant chaplain to the newly established colony of New South Wales; as a magistrate, sought to improve the moral character of a penal society and advocated for better treatment of female convicts; introduced the gospel to the Maoris in New

5. From a popular Victorian journal of the time, *The Home Book for Pleasure and Instruction*, cited in Goodwin, *How To Be A Victorian*, 312.

Zealand as well as education, including vocational and theological training; helped found the first orphanage and branches of both the Bible Society and Church Missionary Society (CMS) in Australia.[6]

Amy also learned that her grandfather John Oxley had come from Yorkshire, at 15 joined the Royal Navy, and was commissioned to chart Australia's coastline; in a short space of time was appointed Surveyor-General of the whole colony, and granted 1,000 (later extended to 5,000) acres of prime farming land south of Sydney; undertook pioneering, at times life-threatening, expeditions in unexplored parts of the country to the west and north; became involved in consolidating schools and orphanages, as well as in the work of the Bible Society; was appointed a magistrate and ultimately one of five members of the first Legislative Council; sadly died aged only 44 as a consequence of the privations and hardships experienced as an explorer.[7]

Amy's parents often socialized with important people who had country homes in the Camden area. These included a Premier of New South Wales, leading sheep farmers in the colony like the MacArthurs,[8] other celebrated explorers, church leaders, and occasionally missionaries, one of whom came from China. At the other end of the social scale, family members also mixed with local Aborigines, who were intermittently employed, and held corroborees, at "Denbigh."

After several years of financial uncertainty due to falling wheat prices and risky capital investment, John reluctantly decided to put most of his property on the market. As Harriet wrote to her sister Marianne, "John owes a great deal of money . . . and really there seems very little chance of him paying it back for some years."[9] The sale took a while, and left John with only enough money to rent a large two-storey house, "Willow Lodge," in Glebe two miles from the center of Sydney. It was a handsome property, built on stone foundations, with brick walls, a slate roof, an elegant verandah, and a small front garden. Inside there were eight apartments that had previously accommodated several adults, domestic servants, and occasional

---

6. On Samuel Marsden see Johnstone, *Samuel Marsden*, and Yarwood, "Samuel Marsden," *ADEB*, 250–53.

7. See Dunlop, "Oxley, John Joseph," accessed March 2016. For detail see Johnson, *Inland Sea*.

8. "Eliza Hassall," *Illawarra Historical Society*, March/April 1999, 29.

9. Letter dated January 1863, as well as others from 11 February and 14 October 1864.

guests. The size and location of "Willow Lodge" opened up the more secure prospect of earning an income making money through offering "genteel" accommodation for short and longer-term lodgers. It would be up to Harriet to manage this, besides looking after a new baby, Beatrice, and five other siblings still at home. Not long after the move, Amy contracted scarlet fever, which was highly contagious and had life-threatening consequences. This early brush with disease was her introduction to sickness and medicine, something that would become a lifetime focus.

At the start of 1875, a new world opened up for Amy. She was now old enough to attend nearby Glebe Public School, the first educational institution in the area that was already gaining a reputation for being progressive. As the school year had only two terms, one in autumn and one in winter, Amy could still spend half of every year at home helping her mother or visiting members of the wider family, especially her Aunt Eliza who lived upriver at Parramatta, the second oldest settlement in the colony. In one of these off-seasons, her aunt Marianne and cousin Isabel visited Sydney from Geelong in the adjacent state of Victoria. The two girls discovered they had much in common, and in the following years their friendship developed by letter and further visits to Sydney.[10]

> By the late 1870s, convict transportation and British military presence had finally ended. Although Queen Victoria's dominant reign had lasted nearly half a century, Australia was developing a more confident pride in its own identity. Every state now had its own elected parliament, and the first moves towards federation of the separate colonies were under way. The eight-hour day had been introduced in the state of Victoria, and significant industries were beginning to develop. Technological innovations, such as incandescent light bulbs, cash registers, antiseptic medical treatments, and overseas telegraph messages, were making an appearance.

In the wake of the Public Instruction Act of 1880, which introduced a uniform curriculum and training of teachers, Amy was invited to become a pupil-teacher in her school. While undertaking a one-year course, trainees were apprenticed to a teacher in the classroom. During the holidays, she and her siblings often stayed in their grandmother Emma Oxley's elegant sandstone residence overlooking Sydney Harbor in the leafy waterside suburb of Hunter's Hill. When Amy was fifteen, Emma's health deteriorated and, except for the eldest children, the family moved from "Willow Lodge"

---

10. See Marianne's letters and diary for October 1879, June 1881, July 1883, and May 1885 in the Hope Family Collection.

to care for her and maintain the estate. Though Amy had to travel to and from Glebe by ferry each day, it was nonetheless an idyllic move. During this time, rowing on the river that bordered the suburb became one of her favorite pastimes. She belonged to a team coached by her father, and, on one occasion, a local newspaper reported that:

> An interesting contest took place on Saturday last, when on the Parramatta River six rowing matches were conducted over a course of half a mile and a good quarter-mile for each of the other events with ladies taking part in each race. In March 1886, the third of a series of similar matches took place in which Miss Amy Oxley (the cox), was the animating spirit.[11]

For Amy, 1886 was a year of decision. She had now been teaching for three years and enjoyed the challenge of learning to communicate with children, especially slower learners. The Sydney Hospital for Sick Children had recently opened in Glebe, and its innovative approach to pediatric care appealed to her interest in both teaching and nursing. The following autumn, now eighteen, she applied to start training. While waiting for the term to begin, Amy wrote to Aunt Marianne asking if she could spend the next few months on her 4,500-acre property in Victoria.

At "Darriwill" Amy "worked for her keep" by acting as a driver for her Aunt Marianne, and helping to improve the tennis court. She also enjoyed riding, swimming, shooting, and even sailing on a nearby river. The extended stay gave her more time with her cousin Isabel, whom in later letters she often referred to as "dear Captain" to whom she was "second mate."[12] Both shared a growing Christian faith and were interested in the spread of the gospel throughout the world.[13] The daily routine at "Darriwill" was bookended by morning and evening prayers, with Bible readings that, according to Australian historian Manning Clark, Amy's second cousin, were attended by the entire household, including the servants.[14] She was keen to attend a variety of interdenominational meetings in the district, some at "Darriwill" itself. Aunt Marianne made the homestead a haven for visiting Christian workers needing a rest, who shared in "parlor meetings" on Sundays. On her nineteenth birthday, Amy received a card from her aunt Eliza encouraging her to visit Rev H. B. Macartney, when she and Marianne next went into Melbourne. Knowing that Amy was already wondering about serving as a nurse overseas,

---

11. See, for example, the later report in the *Sydney Morning Herald*, 30 July 1894, 3.

12. Welch, *Amy Oxley*, accessed January 2015.

13. At the time of Isabel Hope's death in 1939, her personal address book included the details of missionaries from China, India, Japan, Palestine and the New Hebrides.

14. McKenna, *Eye for Eternity*, 55.

her aunt felt that a conversation with this leading supporter of missionary work would help clarify her thoughts about the future.

> From her earliest days at "Denbigh," Eliza Marsden Hassall (1834–1917) assisted her father Thomas, and her brother James, in their ministries. She helped supervise the Sunday School at the church in Cobbitty. Never marrying, she managed the large estate and even learned wine-making. When her father died, Eliza moved with her mother to Parramatta and cared for her until Anne's death. From her early 20s, she was deeply involved in the work of the British and Foreign Bible Society, and in her 40s started the first Australian branch of the Young People's Scripture Union, only a year after it was founded in London. Within a decade, her boundless energy and people skills helped this grow to twelve thousand members across three hundred branches.[15]

In early 1887, Amy returned to Sydney to begin her training in Glebe.[16] The Hospital for Sick Children, the first specifically for children in New South Wales, catered primarily for the children of poor and destitute families, many of whom came from the rural areas.

04 Nurse Amy at Sydney Hospital for Sick Children

---

15. Teale, "Hassall, Eliza Marsden," *ADB*, viewed March 2015; Stewart and Hassall, *Hassall Family*, 79–80.

16. *Town and Country*, April 1875, 44.

Recalling her own brush with death as a child, Amy began learning how to care for children with infectious and other deadly childhood diseases, congenital abnormalities, and conditions caused by malnutrition, as well as those recovering from surgery after accidents. Diphtheria, which had taken a severe toll on children until the invention of a vaccine in the 1920s, dominated the hospital's work at this time.[17] Amy learned the importance of getting to know and treating the children personally. An article, written when she was just twenty-one, gives us a wonderful first-hand glimpse of the kind of person she was and of her approach.

> We should desire, as far as possible, to make our hospitals resemble homes, where soothing influences can add their due weight ... to infuse a return to health. If, then, this kindly attention is of much value to adults, how much more beneficial is it likely to prove to children for whom sympathy in their suffering is almost a first necessity? ... It must be borne in mind that the children cannot describe to us what is amiss; and it is often only by the closest observation and deepest sympathy that we can succeed in ascertaining the cause of pain.[18]

Towards the end of her training, in 1891, her father suddenly collapsed and died. This came as a shock to Amy but strengthened her resolve to make her life count. Only the year before, Hudson Taylor's influential article on the importance of missionary work, "To Every Creature," reached Australia, and in May that year Mary Reed, the first Australian to go as a missionary with the China Inland Mission (CIM), returned and spoke to a near-full audience at the Centennial Hall in Sydney. Her lecture, "Why I Went to China, and What I Saw There," immediately caught Amy's attention, including its "appeal for missionaries who were ready to assist in spreading tidings of the Gospel in the great territory embraced by the Chinese Empire."[19] Hearing that Hudson Taylor's visit was limited to Melbourne later that year, she had to content herself with Eliza and Isabel's reports on how his simplicity and naturalness made his appeal for China more forceful and compelling. In November, however, she was able to meet with the first group of seven Australians going out with CIM, together with Mary Reed, when they passed through Sydney.[20] A series of meetings addressed by the influential Keswick

---

17. In 1904 the institution was renamed the Royal Alexandria Hospital and today is part of the highly regarded Westmead Children's Hospital.
18. *Town and Country* 7 September 1889, 30.
19. From the *Sydney Morning Herald*, 7 June 1890, 19.
20. From Welch, "Mary Reed," August 2014.

Signals of China Calling (1868-1895)

Convention speaker, Rev George Grubb, at her home church, St Barnabas' Broadway, reinforced her conviction of a call to missionary work.[21]

What finally clinched this was the visit in May 1892 of a pioneer CMS missionary from Fukien (Fujian), China, Rev Robert Stewart, accompanied by Eugene Stock, the Society's editorial secretary. In stirring public meetings held at St Andrew's Cathedral, and to hundreds of Chinese Christians in the YCMA Hall, Stewart spoke powerfully about the need in China.

> He held up a graven figure in his hand and described how families in every house prayed to idols like this for their protection. He showed them a very small shoe and explained how infant girls were cruelly hurt and deformed by foot binding. He told of the towers outside cities containing a small hole and pit into which newborn girls were frequently cast. How was God now gathering these people to him? He was working through new day schools, where even girls could now learn to read, write and count, as well as hear stories and sing hymns about Jesus. He was working through new medical centers, which brought healing to countless sick people and the opportunity to hear the gospel and see it in practice. He concluded with an appeal to come and help.[22]

The mention of both medicine and education spoke deeply to Amy. It combined her own convictions and experience. When she heard Stewart and Stock were to visit "Darriwill" as part of a speaking tour of Victoria, she arranged to stay with her cousin while they were there. Amy found Stewart an engaging, down-to-earth, witty person, and even open to her taking his photo! The visitors mentioned that two young women from Melbourne, Nellie and Topsy Saunders, had already offered to go to China with the Church Missionary Association (CMA) Victoria, and would soon join Robert and Louisa Stewart in Kucheng. To her delight, Stock invited Amy to prayerfully consider joining them.[23]

---

21. On Grubb's visit and legacy in Australia see Chant, Spirit of Pentecost, 180–82. Other well-known figures strongly influenced by his missions were Revs R. B. S. Hammond and H. S. Begbie, as well as our grandaunt, Sophie Sackville Newton, whose story is told in Banks, *Faraway Pagoda*.

22. Stewart's extensive influence is discussed in Watson, *Robert and Louisa Watson*, ch. 1.

23. Diary of Marianne Hope, entries dated 10 and 25 August; 9, 12, 13, and 17 September 1892 in the Hope Family Collection.

05 Robert Stewart, in a photo taken by Amy at "Darriwill"

Shortly after she returned to Sydney, Amy applied to the CMA NSW and soon afterwards was accepted. Within the month, her Aunt Eliza was also invited by the Association to found and supervise a missionary training home for women. She offered her own home, "Cluden", a large residence in Ashfield, for the purpose.

06 The Marsden Training Home, with Eliza (sitting, left) and Amy (standing, left), c. 1893.

The Marsden Training Home began operating early in 1893.[24] It was opened by the Dean of Sydney, William Cowper, and dedicated to the memory of Eliza's grandfather, Rev Samuel Marsden. Alongside Amy, the first intake included two other students accepted by the CMA. A grey outfit with a high, starched black collar was their uniform. In the second half of the year, several more women entered the Home. For Amy, living and learning with others was a wonderful experience. The opportunity to devote all her time to studying the Christian faith, sharing with other committed young women, and preparing for missionary work was a special privilege. The program of study included the Bible, church history, and apologetics; practical subjects like mission geography, first aid, and music; and electives on elementary and obstetric nursing. Lectures were given by visiting clergymen and others, including Eliza herself.

During her next two years at the Home, Amy decided to include the course on obstetric nursing, which she passed with honors. This had not been part of her training at the Hospital for Sick Children, but was valuable for work in China.[25] On weekends she developed links with several Chinese churches in Sydney. Finally, on 22 May 1894, the CMA officially appointed Amy to Fukien Province and scheduled her departure for 27 October. This gave her the honor of being the first NSW CMA candidate ever to be sent out to China. Before leaving, she made a trip to "Darriwill," her last opportunity to spend time with Isabel. While there, she learned that because of Japanese aggression against China and hostility against Westerners by some Chinese groups, her departure would be delayed.[26]

Anglican work in Fukien Province began in 1842 through the English CMS. Its growth was slow, partly due to the death of two of its first three missionaries. For a time, Rev John Wolfe, and his Australian wife, carried on the work alone. American Methodists were the other main denomination in the province. All Westerners were required to base their work in the foreign concession outside the Old City of Foochow, (Fuzhou) on Nantai Island. In the 1870s Christianity took root in inland districts, first through CMS in Kucheng (Gucheng), and then through a Chinese pastor in Lieng Kong (Lianjiang). By the mid 1890s, there were still only sixteen Anglican missionaries—eleven clergy, two laymen, and three female teachers—in

---

24. Along with many newspaper descriptions of this event, see *Missionary at Home and Abroad*, March 1893, 8.

25. According to the *Church Missionary Gleaner*, 1 February 1895, 23, some of this took place in the Marsden Training Home itself.

26. An administrative issue that also contributed to the delay is discussed in correspondence between the main stakeholders in Welch, *Amy Oxley*, 1 January 1895 to 18 July 1895.

> a province of twenty million people, with around three thousand baptized members, and an equal number of church attenders.[27]

Until it was safe to travel to Foochow, Amy committed much of her time to what CMA described as "useful work" among its Gleaners' Unions and Sowers Bands.[28] Gleaners' Unions raised money for missionary support and collected items for use by missionaries, such as books and clothing. These were packed and shipped in premises provided by Quong Tart, a well-known leading Christian businessman in the city. Amy resourced and co-ordinated the leaders of these groups, and also helped set up new ones. Sowers Bands were for school-age children who read stories about missionaries, wrote letters to them, and collected items they could use. Amy visited and helped establish these in many churches. She also spoke at larger annual gatherings of children from across the state.[29]

Thursday 1 August 1895 would be forever etched in Amy's heart and life. Waking late after an evening Gleaners' meeting in the city, she was enjoying breakfast on her own when Aunt Eliza walked into the room ashen-faced and visibly shaking. From under her arm she placed the morning newspaper on the table, open at some shocking news. Six days earlier, Amy's soon-to-be colleagues, Robert and Louisa Stewart, two of their younger children, the Saunders sisters and another Australian, and four other missionaries, had been brutally murdered by an anti-Western society in the hills above Kucheng. The severity of this event made headline news in major newspapers all around the world.[30]

---

27. Tang, "Mission in China," 1–3, accessed April 2016, and Cole, *Church Missionary Society*, 43–44. The best account of the development of Christianity in China during these years is provided in Bays, *Christianity in China*, 46–91.

28. CMA Report, 1894, 6.

29. *Evening News*, 7 December 1895, 5.

30. This was a precursor of the wider, more organized, Boxer Movement that a few years later resulted in the deaths of hundreds of missionaries and thousands of Chinese converts. See Welch, "The Vegetarians," 468–83. We have provided a fuller account of the massacre, including its background and aftermath, in Banks, *Through the Valley* 10–22.

07 Kucheng martyrs' graves on Nantai Island, Foochow

Amy was grief-stricken. Only a few days earlier she had received a letter from Louisa Stewart in Hwasang saying that, though there were stirrings among a group of organized agitators, the work was going well.[31] As a result of media coverage, the event had a similar impact to major terrorist attacks today, and was the subject of everyday conversations in ferries and trains, shops and tearooms, workplaces, and dinner parties. Articles began appearing in the press about the "waste" of the young women's lives, some going as far to say that "it was a crime to send female missionaries" to places like China.[32] In response to this, Nellie and Topsy's mother spoke movingly at a memorial service in St Paul's Cathedral, Melbourne:

> Was it right to send our young women out to foreign countries as missionaries? Since men could only do certain kinds of work, who was going to rescue and save the suffering women? If I had two or even ten more daughters, I would gladly give them up to work in China.[33]

A few days later, on 16 August, Amy gave expression to her continuing resolution to serve in China in a talk on "The Love of God as the Great Missionary Motive Power."[34] Though she was still a little apprehensive, as soon as word came that it was safe for her to depart, Amy prepared to go.

31. As reported in *The Age*, 7 August 1895, 5.
32. *Illawarra Mercury*, 13 August 1895, 2.
33. *The Age*, 19 August 1895, 7.
34. *Cumberland Free Press*, 24 August 1895, 4.

2

The Blind Boy in the Ditch (1896–1900)

IN EARLY OCTOBER 1895, Amy received a telegraph letter from the CMS in London.

> You will, we assume, ere long be on your way to Hong Kong. There our Secretary, Mr Bennett, will meet you, and I can assure you of a warm welcome there from both Mr and Mrs Bennett. They will arrange for all hospitality to be afforded you until the way opens for your going on to Foochow.[1]

After waiting for more than a year, Amy now had less than two months to get everything organized to leave and say her goodbyes. It seemed like no time at all before her farewell service took place on 10 December, followed by her departure the next day.

> A Valedictory communion service was held at St Andrew's Cathedral, Sydney, this morning in connection with the approaching departure of Miss Amy Oxley, who has decided upon entering missionary work in China. There was a fairly large number of communicants and friends at the service, which was conducted by the Rev William Martin BA of St Barnabas' Glebe and the Rev R. J. Reid of St Andrew's.[2]

---

1. This letter was written by Rev S. Baring Gould, secretary of CMS in London. It, along with all the following letters without references, are drawn from Welch, *Amy Oxley*; and may be located in the chronological ordering of the correspondence.

2. *Evening News*, 22 December 1895, 4.

> The China Navigation Company's steamer, "Chingtu," left the company's wharf, Milson's Point . . . Miss Oxley is going as missionary for the Church Missionary Society and a short service was held on board by her friends before the vessel left. There were present . . . members of the Missionary Gleaner's Union, and a number of ladies and gentlemen interested in the work. Several Chinese and Kanaka converts also attended. The Rev M. Archdall delivered a short address; Rev W. Martin offered prayer after an appropriate hymn had been sung and the service concluded with the Benediction.[3]

Over the next few years, Amy provided various personal accounts of what she was doing. Many of these were personal letters to her cousin Isabel in Australia. Others were more formal reports to CMS officials in London or to another Christian organization; some were correspondence with or from friends or colleagues. A few come from reports in newspapers or magazines. Since we have so many first-hand accounts of her activities, we can tell most of what happened during this in her own, or her contemporaries' words.

Letter to Isabel, 22 December 1895:

> I never write letters on Sunday but as I will have the opportunity of posting this to you at Port Darwin I will alter my rule for once. I hopped up on my bunk, put my hand in my mailbag and drew out a letter from you. Thank you so very much for it and for the enclosed verses which I will keep in my Bible. My bag contained 65 letters and a packet for Christmas so I am well off. It is a real joy getting these letters every day . . .
>
> So far we have had a beautiful passage and I have not even had a headache. I feel sure God is answering prayer. At first on board there wasn't one soul who cared for Missions but now Praise the Lord things are different. I find the second officer was on board the "Haitian" and was one of the officers who gave the Saunders [sisters] the "kitten." I have lent him their letters to read and he is very interested . . . I have found Jesus sufficient for everything. All the pain of saying goodbye . . . He is faithful to His promise, so I am with you.
>
> There are only three men, two ladies and two boys as passengers. Four of them did not get on till we reached Thursday Island. I think I will like them. At first the young lady, Miss Swann, scorned me but we are quite good friends now, although she is not willing to give up the world and take Jesus Himself. The officers are exceedingly kind to me. Captain Innes travelled

---

3. *Evening News*, 11 December 1895, 7.

with [my brother] Willie in the "Tainan"... It has been 90 [degrees] all the time in my Cabin, now I find it difficult to write for my hand clings to the paper. With all my heart's love to you and dear Auntie.

Letter to Rev Baring Gould, secretary of CMS, London, 17 January 1896, mentioning the CMS Secretary in Asia, a fellow-Australian :

> I arrived at Hong Kong at the end of January and stayed there one week. Mr and Mrs Bennett were exceedingly kind and gave me every opportunity of seeing the work. On the 10th, I left Hong Kong arriving in Foochow on the 14th... Thank you very much for sending me a copy of the General Instructions, also for the Books of Rules and Regulations. I trust I may be a faithful worker in this part of the Mission Field that the Master has called me to work in.

08 Old City of Foochow, looking up towards Kuliang (Guliang)

Kuliang was a village in the scenic mountain range overlooking Foochow. It took four hours to reach by walking or by sedan chair. A medical missionary was the first to set up a house there to escape the summer heat. Many Western expatriates and organizations followed, including missionary societies. During the hot months of July and August, the CMS held its main annual conference and convention in the village, while participants rented—and occasionally built—houses there. Among Kuliang's facilities were a social club, tennis court, swimming pool, and hiking tracks. It provided an opportunity for missionaries to catch up with each other, share news from home and relax in a beautiful setting.

Letter to Isabel from the "Go-Down," a warehouse with guest rooms used by different missions, on Nantai Island, Foochow, 19 February 1896:

> Early on January 14th we reached the Min River and steamed up to the Anchorage. It was a dull cold morning but I stood on the deck looking at everything ... high mountains on either side with terraces. We passed dozens of junks and sampans on the river and very picturesque they looked ...
>
> On the afternoon of my arrival a conference of ladies was held and I was appointed to work in the Lieng Kong district. It is a very large place, a city and many villages. Although there is a native pastor there and work being carried on, there has been no resident missionary ... I hardly expect to go there till I have passed my first exam in about a year ... Lieng Kong is a day's journey from Foochow and the Foochow dialect is spoken there ...
>
> *Climate*: It has been cold enough for thick dresses (my Geelong tweed is most comfortable), hot bottle in bed, two blankets and an eiderdown. One day we had snow but every day it has been dull and cold, most days raining.
>
> *Houses*: Large rooms, high with French windows, verandas with shutters all round.
>
> *Food*: Almost the same as at home only buffalo milk and butter which is pure white in colour and something like very nice lard. Vegetables in season: cabbage, cauliflower, carrots, potatoes. Fruit: oranges and tasteless bananas. Most of the missionaries send home for groceries and I will do the same. Things are too dear out here.
>
> *Conveyances*: Chairs carried by two or three coolies. Just cane armchairs made any size you like, with a cover to fit on something like a cage with windows at the side. Bamboo poles are fastened on the side of the chair. Walks mostly on the hills among the gravestones. All the hills here are covered with graves and pretty little ferns grow on the ledges of the old stone ones. Then there are a very few narrow roads made by the English residents, and there are also narrow paths across the "paddy-fields ..."

Church: There is a Church of England service conducted by the Rev L Lloyd of our mission, also Chinese service at [Trinity] College, the Rev Sinke is the pastor, a really splendid man.

Language: It is difficult and I do need the grace of God to learn it. I have a teacher, Ding Sing Ang, and I study between four and five hours a day. No one does more without in the end breaking down. It makes me feel very tired and not inclined for letter writing.

I am so glad I am here, every day I feel more glad.

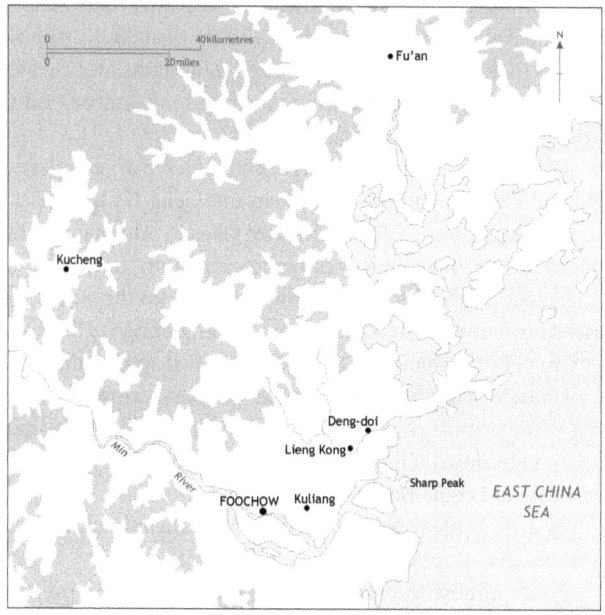

09 Map of central Fukien Province

Letter to the Young Women's Christian Association, Sydney, 3 April 1896:

> I am so glad to be in China, for I begin to see how much these people need Jesus . . . when you come to a land like this and see the women either shut up in houses in pain or ill health from their little bound feet or else field women who have to work hard from morning till night, carry very heavy baskets full of refuse, or working in the fields up to their knees in mud and water, it is then you see and realize the difference between a Heathen and a Christian land—again the hopelessness of the people, no joy in the life to come, no joy for the ones left here because the spirits of the departed ones will come back and torment them if they

are not fed, paper money put on their graves and crackers let off at certain times of the year . . .

I saw three field women and two men come to a grave, and they offered incense, put money about, dug up the earth and then went away, leaving one woman there by herself; there she stood in the drizzling rain, moaning and moaning . . . I knew not how much sorrow really filled her heart, but I know this that I just longed to go and tell her of the Saviour . . . Poor things, the men came back after a while and tried to draw her away, but she would not leave . . . from my window I can see thousands and thousands of graves and it is overwhelming to think of the wailing that has gone on year after year and to think of those who have passed into the great unknown . . . one thing about them—the Judge of all the earth shall do right.[4]

Letter to Isabel after Amy's appointment to Lieng Kong with two other single female missionaries, 19 November 1896:

> In the last few weeks I have had about a hundred patients . . . This has been a sad time for the Chinese. With the long continued hot weather and no rain there have been hundreds ill with fever, boils, and some have died of the plague, but now we have had a good shower of rain and the weather is cooler. I had enlarged liver and thin liver for a few days but I am well again now. I hope to pass my first exam in January.

Letter to Mrs Margaret Griffiths, daughter of the Anglican archbishop of Sydney, Right Rev William Saumarez Smith, 6 April 1898:

> In January we moved to our new house in Deng Doi, which is a village of 2000 families six miles from Lieng Kong City. Miss Newton was appointed by Conference to the District and so we three, Miss Searle, Miss Newton and I live together and very happy we are. Our nearest Missionary neighbor is 30 miles away . . . This is a large District about 40 miles from one end to the other and 35 miles across, high mountains to cross, rivers to travel up and a long coastline.
>
> I see sick people and have at least 160 a week [in her dispensary], some we have to turn away it is so sad . . . We really do need . . . a Hospital and a Doctor, two days a week. We are so

4. *Scrutineer and Berrima District Press*, 17 June 1896, 2.

thankful that some women here are beginning to see the sin of foot binding, two have unbound their feet and some more are making shoes.[5]

Excerpts from a report by a colleague on the commencement of the work at Deng Doi, mentioning one of Amy's colleagues.

> "The people received us with joy," wrote Miss Oxley, "and were invited to so many feasts that we had to ask them not to invite us to any more, as we really had not time to spend in this way." Many of the visitors were interested . . . in the foreign-looking Mission house . . . nicely situated on a hill above . . . the village below, yet conveniently near. "It is a real house," writes Miss Searle, "to which we always come back after a long itinerating tour with the intensest gratitude and delight" . . .
>
> There are villages all around Deng Doi . . . Miss Oxley, who shares in the itinerating, is an accomplished "master mariner" . . . she is the owner and commander of "The Messenger of Peace," with its dinghy, "The Active," the latter being named after the craft in which the Rev Samuel Marsden, the apostle of New Zealand, journeyed.[6]

10 Amy in dinghy alongside *The Messenger of Peace*

---

5. In Welch, *Amy Oxley*, this piece of correspondence appears to be wrongly dated a year earlier.

6. "A Little Australian Colony," *Bowral Free Press*, 10 May 1900, 4.

As was customary, the local people devised a Chinese name for Amy. This was made up of three characters: the first of these, her surname, meant "high mountain"; the last two were similar to the pronunciation of her first name. These meant, respectively, "love," "fondness," or "affection," and "beautiful" or "good." The practice of giving such a name was both more convenient for the people and a sign of acceptance.

The China that Amy was now heading to was marked by deep contradictions. Though it was a vast country, for most of its inhabitants their world was an area bounded by their own village, town, or city. Its four hundred million inhabitants were diverse in culture and divided by language and dialect. They were ruled by the imperial Qing Dynasty, whose present Emperor Guangxu had been on the throne for twenty-two years. In reality, the lives of ordinary people were mostly under the sway of local warlords who from time to time defied the central authorities. Chinese in positions of influence were mostly well-off, but the majority of people were often poor and at the mercy of natural disasters. The influence of ethical teachers, like Confucius, and imported religions, such as Buddhism, was strong, but in rural areas ancestor worship and local deities were alive and well.

> For centuries China had developed as a world to itself. The main exceptions to this were the opening up of the Silk Road from the West, the journey of the Italian explorer Marco Polo, and the arrival of Jesuit missionaries from the middle of the sixteenth century. This isolation began to change with the British East India Company's willful decision to sell opium to the Chinese. When, in the early 1840s, the Chinese rejected this, Britain declared war and, after a short campaign, demanded large financial reparations and use of five key ports—Hong Kong, Canton, Shanghai, Ningpo, and Foochow. Over the next few decades, Britain, other European powers, and the United States forcibly obtained trading rights in numerous cities throughout China. Beyond these enclaves, Western influence extended inland through the railways, river steamers, and telegraph stations.[7]

Like the rest of the country, Lieng Kong District suffered from some major social problems:

---

7. For a brief account of Western and Chinese relationships in this period see Keen, *Short History of China*, 2–13, 101–11, and more fully in Hsu, *Modern China*, 262–352.

- *opium addiction.* Like modern-day heroin, this had grown exponentially since the introduction of the opium trade. Increasingly it rendered men unable to work and exposed poor families to debt. Sometimes this affected whole villages.[8]

- *infanticide.* Because of the Chinese dowry system, girls were considered an economic liability, especially among the poorer classes, and were often abandoned after birth. Some were left in public places, others exposed in the countryside, many deposited into pillar boxes above a river. Disabled children of both sexes, including the blind, often suffered the same fate.

- *foot-binding.* As arranged marriages were customary in China, and small feet in females considered more attractive, among the upper classes foot-binding was practiced to make them more marketable. From four or five years old, major bones in the feet were broken and twisted into specially made lotus-shaped shoes that permanently cramped their development. While a few educated or religious Chinese had begun to oppose this practice, up to half of all Chinese girls were affected by it.[9]

- *lack of schooling.* Since girls were regarded mainly as household help and future child-bearers, educating them was not considered to be economically worthwhile. As a consequence, where schools were established they were primarily for boys, and professions were almost exclusively reserved for men.

During her first year in Deng Doi, Amy's eyes were opened to the possibility of a new dimension to her work. The following is a pastiche of accounts about how this happened.

> In [my] homeland, I had passed the blind on the other side of the street, for I had no special interest in them. Now my heart was stirred to its depths on many occasions when blind children were brought to me in our dispensary. What could I do? The answer I received from a small boy when I asked how he received a bruise on his face. "Oh my uncle just struck me in the face and said: 'Get out of my way, you blind boy'" . . .

---

8. For southern China, see Lee, *Bible and the Gun*, and on the opium trade and its consequences, Lovell, *Opium War*.

9. There is a detailed description of foot-binding a very young girl in the children's book by Codrington, *Bring-Brother*, 39–41. Further background on the practice is provided by Paddle, *Itinerario*, 67–82.

> Going to a village one day, I stumbled across a helpless blind boy cowering in a ditch. He told me his father had wanted to kill him but seeing I was coming, had left him for me . . .
>
> An appeal made to me by a woman for her only son in the little mission church of Lieng Kong. "He is my only son. I am a widow, and he is blind: do good deeds, open his eyes and give him to see." Alas! his sight was beyond restoring, and the fact left a lasting impression on my mind. To be blind is a terrible thing. To be blind of poor Chinese parentage is still more terrible. My sympathy was drawn out as I thought about them being blind of God's beauteous world around and blind of Heaven's own light![10]

Amy was aware that Chinese children had a greater tendency to contract blindness.[11] This was brought about by a number of factors, such as vitamin A deficiency, trachoma, glaucoma, congenital cataracts, accidents, and measles. Lack of adequate medical treatment escalated the problem. Among more well-to-do Chinese, sightless people were sometimes encouraged to become respected fortune tellers, musical performers, or administrators. The general desire to know the most propitious times for betrothals, marriages, funerals, business deals, or journeys enabled a minority of blind people, primarily men, to forge some kind of living for themselves. However, the oversupply of blind street musicians and ballad singers trying to make a living, meant that most of these remained little more than beggars.[12]

In a further collection of accounts, Amy goes on to describe how she responded to this challenge. After a severe typhoon in Lieng Kong, she was evacuated to the port of Amoy (now Xiamen) further down the coast.

> During September 1898 there was a terrible typhoon, and our kitchen and servants quarters were almost destroyed, only one room in the house remained undamaged . . .
>
> God opened a "door"—and I was invited to visit a blind school in the Amoy district. Miss Graham of the English Presbyterian Mission had brought out to Amoy a blind Scotsman,

---

10. This, and the following, group of quotes are a composite drawn from materials in which Amy recounted her call to work with the blind, including a letter to Margaret Griffith, Welch, *Amy Oxley*, 6 April 1897 (actually 1898); *Church Missionary Gleaner*, 1 May 1900, 36–38; *Soul-Lighted School of Foochow*, Wilkinson, "School for Blind Boys"; and an article by her for the *Berrima District Historical Society*, written after 1923.

11. Of an estimated one million blind children presently in Asia, around 40 percent live in China. See 'Public Health Issue'.

12. Miles, *Disability and Dialogue*.

Mr Cooke, to try to teach the blind Chinese. It was he who showed me English Braille...

With the help of the grace of God, I was [the first] to adapt the Braille system to the romanized version of our Foochow dialect [in which parts of the Bible were already translated]. This was a great improvement and the British and Foreign Bible Society agreed to print the Epistle to the Romans and the Prayer Book version of the Psalms for us...

Returning to the Lieng Kong district I rented a tiny native house in one of the dirty streets of Deng Doi, approached by a cobblestone path, up some very uneven steps. This contained my school room, 2 feet by 8 feet, just long enough for a table, two chairs, and a form. On either side was a bedroom, 8 feet by 10 feet, and outside a shed which served as a kitchen and dining room combined. Then, with an old cook, I opened my School for the Blind...

Well do I remember sitting in that tiny school room and teaching my first boy.[13]

That first boy, Xiao Nin Kai, was the only son of the widow who had earlier appealed for her help, and he was destined to become a significant figure in the work she had begun.

> The complex Chinese writing system—containing more than four thousand individual characters—made anything to do with language extremely difficult for the blind. Though some embossed Bibles and religious books had appeared in the mid 1800s, a form of Braille was first introduced by a missionary to Peking in 1879. As this was based on numerical equivalents for each character, it took a long time to learn and was complicated to use. The development of a more alphabetic equivalent for the sounds of the characters—built on so-called initials and finals roughly corresponding to consonant and vowel sounds—gradually followed. Amy's was the first school to render the Foochow dialect into Braille. In this, each syllable required two or more Braille dots.

---

13. For details of these quotes, see footnote 44. In the brief self-published account by the school of its development, *Fu Zhou Shi Mang Xiao*, 4, the place Amy rented is described as a farmhouse.

The Blind Boy in the Ditch (1896–1900)

Alongside starting to teach the blind, Amy continued to be involved in her regular missionary work with her colleagues.

From an article in the *Church Missionary Gleaner*, describing the character of the work in Deng Doi:

> As we were the first 'kuniongs' [single women] to live in this city the people were anxious to see our house, and numbers came in every day. We trust that the Word that was preached to them may take deep root in their hearts and bring forth fruit.
>
> A few people asked for medicine and when they found that it did them good they told their friends and relatives, with the result that for days hundreds of people came: we limited the number to eighty or ninety a day, women and children only. Wherever we went in the street or villages some poor creatures would beseech us to look at their sore leg, or eye or something. A poor widow mother would bring her only son, and he hopelessly blind. A brother would bring his leper sister, and beg us to do something for her, and one day some men carried their mother from a village nine miles distant, and the poor thing died of cancer.
>
> It is possible here to have an audience at a few moment's notice and open the church doors and then play some hymns on the baby-organ, and in come all sorts and conditions from the proudest man in the long blue coat to the dirtiest child imaginable and the people will listen by the hour while the gospel is preached to them . . . The people are very willing to receive us into their homes, and there are more invitations than we can accept.[14]

Letter to Isabel (mentioning Nellie and Topsy Saunders' mother, who was now a self-supporting CMS missionary serving in Fukien Province) 27 February 1898:

> This week I went to Sien O with Mrs. Saunders. We had a grand day. The Devil tried to hinder by upsetting the coolies along the road and it ended in me walking the 3 miles and then later on the chair pole broke and we had great work to tie it up. At Sien O hundreds heard the Gospel, over 15 children gave their names as willing to attend day school. Over 20 sick people were treated and a family publicly burned their idols. Our hearts were thankful.

---

14. *Church Missionary Gleaner*, 1 March 1900, 36.

We have a new Catechist, one who has been Miss Searle's teacher for two years and he will be a real help to us and the people. The new church is begun, also the Women's School. There are six boys in the Blind School, all getting on well. Your little Ning Kai, who has written you a letter and made you a pair of cuffs is the best boy. I do thank God for him, I am now teaching him to play the organ.

Letters to Isabel and Aunt Marianne at "Darriwill," 7 and 11 May 1898 respectively:

My dear Isabel,

I have just received an invitation to go to a wedding . . . I went to the feast with S. Newton but we had some dinner immediately before we started. The house we went to is not very grand. Just inside the front door there is a room with an earth floor and various tubs, fishing nets, etc., all about. The next room is like it but today had two square tables spread ready for the feast . . . here were about eight saucers full of things, in two dried fish, in two watermelon seeds. We were invited to sit down and the bride was brought out of the bedroom for us to look at. Poor thing, she was not allowed to speak and she did look miserable, her hair was covered with ornaments and she had on a red dress. After standing for us to gaze at she was turned to face the wall and left standing in that position.

The eating soon began and it was not really bad, we were not pressed to eat, the Bride sat at the other (inferior) table and was not given anything to eat. After about an hour and a half it was over. I was glad because it is tiring sitting so long not talking, and four dirty hungry dogs under the table all the time is not pleasant. We came to this feast because they are all Christians except the bride, three members were baptised lately. We were invited into the bride's bedroom and then contrary to custom talked. The Bride had a sore foot and asked for medicine and so I sent up for some at once. I do pray that the friendship begun today may grow into love in the Lord.

My dearest Auntie,

All day I have been down at the Blind School . . . it is so very wonderful, the way the Lord has given me this work to do and how gently He has led me on from step to step, not with a great bound that would frighten me. The next step I am in the dark about, how to manage every day housekeeping on so much per month, each boy ought only to cost a certain amount.

Report from fellow-missionary Miss Little about a visit to Deng Doi, 1 July 1898:

> I wonder if those in the homeland know what an enormous district Lieng Kong is, in which their three representatives, Miss Oxley, Miss Newton and Miss Searle are the only resident foreigners . . . Miss Oxley is Senior Missionary . . . there is the medical work twice a week, with an average of at least eighty patients each time. The patients have numbers distributed to them when the gate is opened, and are seen in turn. Preaching goes on before and during the dispensing. God is blessing the remedies used to heal many; and there are signs of spiritual results too . . .
>
> There are two day schools in this village . . . Miss Oxley has a women's class on Tuesday and Sunday afternoons, which one of the others takes when she is itinerating. She had the joy of seeing 11 women, whom she had been preparing for some time, baptized in the chapel last Sunday.[15]

This small church in Deng Doi had been funded almost exclusively by donations from CMA supporters in New South Wales, Victoria and Tasmania.

Letter from Amy in *The Church Missionary Gleaner*, 1 November 1898:

> At the Leper Asylum [in Foochow], I saw a man with a glory and a brightness on his face, that could not possibly have been there unless God had been shining upon him. There are two tiny places where the eyes had been, for now he is blind; there is a small round hole, where once there was a nose; his lips are drawn far apart, and both top and bottom rows of teeth were showing, and yet I have never seen such a wonderful face; for truly love, joy, and perfect peace are written there . . . I have never realized in quite the same way before, how very wonderful is the grace of God, and how His indwelling Presence can so wonderfully transform a human being.[16]

Letter to Isabel, 16 November 1898:

> I just long for you to see the Blind boy and the School cook that you are supporting. Ning Kai . . . has a very sweet face. It just shines with the Peace of God, for he is a true little Christian. His mother died when he was about four years old. He went blind at five and his father died when he was seven. I do not know what his life was like then but last year he went to a place called Ceng

---

15. *Church Missionary Gleaner*, 1 July 1898, 55.
16. *Church Missionary Gleaner*, 1 November 1898, 84.

Song and there an uncle has been feeding him and . . . a Bible-woman . . . has been teaching him. It was such a pleasure to see him before eating his rice fold his hands together and thank God for it . . . I never thought I should have anything to do with the Blind, and here I am really teaching them and loving to do it.

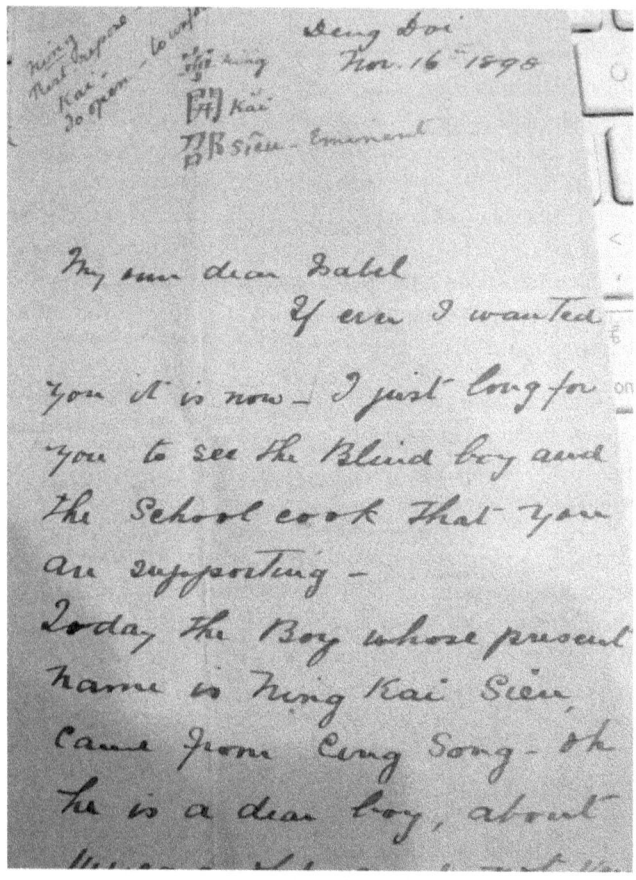

11 Handwritten letter to Isabel, 16 November 1898

Letter to a friend, Margaret Griffith, 18 January 1899:

> Just at present we are having a time of great blessing. The women who were baptized last year are really beginning to see the sin of foot binding and really it is beautiful the way they are unbinding in spite of the pain and the ridicule of the neighbors . . .
> I am more than pleased with the success of the Braille. Some of the boys are learning to knit. I am thinking of sending a little packet of writing etc. to the [CMS] Loan Exhibition as it

The Blind Boy in the Ditch (1896–1900)

will make the work better known and we do need prayer and funds. Perhaps some of your Sunday School members will help in this work by prayer and by giving money. Wool would be very acceptable as the boys are learning to knit. Later on some of them will earn money this way . . .

There is much one wants, yea, longs to do but there is work enough to keep dozens employed. We never have time to spend the evening together. Often I have to remind myself that the work must not take all the time. God First. Without Him what can we do? I shall be so glad to hear from you again. In two more years I expect I will be leaving for Sydney, how very quickly the time passes.

12 Amy, Minna (left), Sophie (middle), and the Bible class at Deng Doi

Letter to Isabel, 30 April 1899:

> God is working in a most wonderful way here just now. The Women's School is full with 26 women. The Blind School full with 15 boys . . . We attend about 60 patients a week just now. Last week on making up the Books I find we have registered the names of 1195 patients.

Two letters, a few days apart, to Isabel, 11 and 15 May 1899:

> Our beautiful new church is nearly finished and the school for women will be finished in August. Oh there is such a wonderful

difference in this place compared to this time last year. Then it seemed nothing but misunderstanding and trials, nearly empty church, etc. Now full old church and real love within people. We had the Bishop here for a Sunday. He confirmed 52 men and women. Some of them were from other villages. 84 partook of the Lord's Supper. Several families lately have given up their idols, it seems as if God has let me see Him working, it is wonderful.

O Bel, I do long to be more full of God's Holy Spirit, and there is such a lot of daily sin to be confessed. One thing I often fail in and that is hasty words, often indignations that I have no right under any circumstances to speak hastily. These sick people often make me completely out of patience with them. Perhaps I have and with much care and trouble succeeded in washing clean a wound, an abscess that has been filled with earth, and in four days it is really beginning to improve, to find the patient does not turn up. Then he comes again hand filled with mud!!! And expects me to go through everything again. Then my nerves seem to tingle and I tell him what a goose he is. And then I wish I hadn't.

Then the coolness of these people making use of our things without asking or by your leave. Just fancy, a family here had diphtheria. Father and daughter died. Very quickly other people who went in to have a look have died. Then a little boy got it and just as he was dying his mother carried him to the Blind School and laid him on one of the beds. The boys were at dinner and a knock came to the door. Ning Kai opened it and could not see who came in but the cook etc. hearing a cough went to see and found this boy. All were terrified as they think it is the plague. The brother was made to take the boy away, he died almost at once, and up they came for me. Of course they were comforted and the matting he was laid on was burnt and the bed washed, but I cannot help being a little anxious . . . But these boys are in the Heavenly Father's keeping and I must not worry.

My own Dear Captain,

I said to Long Hie, one of the small boys, what shall I do, can I stay the night here. He thought for a time and then said, "I don't know which bed you would sleep on." Nor I, for the place is packed and two boys are sleeping in another house which I do not like. More boys want to come and I am looking out for another house—none near at hand to let. One rambling house for sale at 700 dollars = £70, but I hope later on to build. God has begun this work. He sees and knows our need and He will surely supply it in His own time.

A general letter to missionaries in Fukien from Rev B. Baring Gould, which would have future significance for Amy, 18 June 1899:

> It is with strong satisfaction that we write to inform you that at length the Committee have appointed a medical man to open up a Medical Mission in the city of Foochow. Dr Wilkinson, an M.A. and M.B. of Cambridge, who has had some ten years in medical practice, and some experience of Medical Missions in England, will we hope, sail for Foochow with Mr Carpenter, on Oct. 5th. And we trust that a long and useful career of Medical Mission work lies before him in that city. We recognize how hearty will be the welcome offered to him by all the brethren inasmuch as this has been a project which has been for years in the hearts of so many . . . Meanwhile, we would ask you and the other brethren to join with us in earnest prayer that this new development may be abundantly used of God to the extension of His kingdom, not only in Foochow but throughout the Province.

Letter to Isabel, 9 October 1899:

> You ask what you could send the boys for Christmas. Well, it is a little late for Christmas but I do not think anything would please them better than some flannelette to make them a warm jacket. It gets very cold here in January and February with snow last year. I cannot tell you how many yards to send but perhaps there is a remnant not so good, and I will have it made into jackets as far as it will go . . .
>
> Just think, I have been nearly four years in China, such very happy years I can never, never tell how happy. You say, "I wonder sometimes how you have the heart to go on with your work." Well, it isn't very often I feel like that . . . on the other hand we are full of joy, the Women's School really opened with 14 women and more to come.

Report from Minna Searle, 1 November 1899:

> Miss Oxley started in chairs in drizzling rain . . . We were to go to a village on the sea-shore, and there to meet her boat in which she was going to visit three or four villages, and then send it up to Foochow for repairs. The Lord gave her this boat, and it has been so much used in His work, though I don't think very many help to support it. The Lord kept the feet of our coolies and they

brought us through "lovely scenery" to our destination. On the way we passed through a village not one foreign woman had been in before . . . We learn what it is to be 'a spectacle' to men and we must look even funnier to them than they to us, for they have never seen Europeans, even in pictures.[17]

13 Early students at the Blind Boys School

Letter to Isabel, 16 February 1900:

> Of course now the [Boer] War is going on we long to hear all we can about it. I do not have much time for reading but odd half hours I do like to know what is going on in the world. And another thing I think often missionaries' nerves give way so that they never think of anything but their especial little corner and little worries . . .
>
> The boys, 12 now, all did so well at their examinations. Nin Kai . . . can now play 27 hymns beautifully. He has written the whole of St Luke's and part of St John's Gospel, the New Testament Picture Bible and many other things. He . . . has one great sin, and that is pride. He is naturally very upright and often judges others wrongfully without really finding out the whole story. But he knows his fault and is I believe really praying about it . . .
>
> I am expecting 3 more boys and now this house is full I do not know what God is going to do for us . . . There was a thief at the Blind School last night, stole a few clothes and a neighbor's

---

17. Ibid., 1 November 1899, 189–90.

fowl. Fortunately someone awoke and found the thief but could not catch him.

Letter to Isabel, 30 April 1900:

> Last week I had great trouble about the Blind School. A young fellow and some women came in the evening and knocked on the door. Ning Kai opened it and was dragged out and hit in the side with a bamboo. There was a tremendous row and it took such a time enquiring into it. Then the thing was supposed to be settled and I went off for the day to a village . . . While I was away the [blind] boys went off to beat the boy. Oh dear, it was such work to settle it all again.
>
> Two more of the boys want to be baptized and one of them has given me great joy. I think he is truly converted. Seventeen boys now, we do need your prayers.

Report in a country newspaper, 16 May 1900:

> It is a difficult thing to set each blind boy to really work. Each one is supposed to work at some trade half the day, and learn to read and write (Braille System) the remainder. I have set them to work at matting, making string and rope, knitting, and straw shoes.[18]

Before Amy was due to leave on her first furlough, events in China dramatically intervened. The so-called Boxer Rebellion, which had its roots in previous anti-Western movements, of which the Vegetarian attack on Hwasang was a precursor, broke out in northern China. This latest uprising sought to overthrow the Qing Dynasty, attack foreign influence and religions, and kill or at least expel all foreigners. In early 1900, mobs attacked mission stations, several missionaries were killed, and thousands of Chinese converts skinned, hacked, or burned to death. The situation was further inflamed by the dowager empress' proclamation supporting the uprising. A third of a million Boxers, with support from elements in the Chinese Army, besieged more than one thousand Westerners and three thousand Chinese Christians for fifty-five days in Peking.[19]

---

18. *Bowral Free Press*, 16 May 1900.
19. Preston, *Boxer Rebellion*.

While there were little signs of unrest in the district of Lieng Kong, in late June the viceroy and British consul ordered all missionaries from the interior into Foochow. On 1 July there was a further edict from Peking ordering the expulsion of all foreigners from China and the persecution of native Christians. News came from other parts of Fukien Province about property being plundered, people beaten, and one person killed. A few days later there were fears of protesters marching from the old city across the Min River to the foreign concession on Nantai Island, but providentially heavy rain flooded approaches to the bridge.[20]

While Australians waited for news about "Imperilled Australian Missionaries in China," with photos of Amy and others in Fukien, on 23 July the British Consul in Foochow was able to guarantee their safety. Two weeks later, a twenty-thousand-strong international force finally reached the foreign legations in Peking, and by 14 August the siege was over. It was later estimated that the Boxers had killed more than two hundred forty missionaries, three-quarters of them Protestants, and around eight thousand Chinese Christians, the majority of them Catholics.

During this time, Amy had a number of loose ends to tie up in preparation for her furlough. While a replacement was coming to the dispensary, no one was able to carry on her work with the blind boys. As a result, the School did not open in the second half of 1900 and she had to find funds to the cost of appropriate lodging for the students during her absence. This caused her considerable anxiety and sleepless nights.[21] In the midst of this, she was already planning the next stage of her work.

Amy's final letter to Isabel on 16 May 1900:

> It is decided that on my return from Furlough I take up this work among the Blind and devote all my time to it. A school large enough to accommodate 100 boys and a dwelling house for myself and fellow-worker, if one offers for this work, are to be erected in Foochow and one of the married men missionaries will help us in any way we need. An account of the work is to be written and sent to friends asking them to help in collecting money for the building and supporting the boys. In the meantime we ask you to pray definitely that God will guide us in all our plans for the future, and that every detail may be done in a way that will glorify Him.

---

20. For incidents in Fukien Province, see Stock, *Christ and Fuh-kien*, 37.

21. More generally, Amy refers to her tiredness in letters to Isabel on 26 May 1899, 9 October 1899, and 16 February 1900.

3

Surprises of the Heart
(1901–1906)

AMY'S SEA VOYAGE TO Sydney helped her begin the process of unwinding from six years of exhausting work in China. Readjusting to life in Australia made her increasingly aware of how much she had changed. Culture shock, as we call it today, soon hit her hard. Despite regular letters, to her surprise even her own family could only relate to her experiences in a limited way, especially at wider occasions such as weddings and Christmas festivities.[1] On deputations, she found churches were more interested in "exotic stories," especially anything connected to the Boxer Uprising, than the daily challenges of missionary life. Alongside this, she was also missing her colleagues and Chinese friends.

On New Year's Day 1901, halfway through her furlough, Amy took part in celebrations marking Australia's Federation, which united six separate self-governing British colonies into a Commonwealth. However, for Amy, this was tempered by the introduction on the same day of the White Australia Policy, which sought to preference Anglo-Celtic or European immigrants over "non-white" people. Its insistence on a dictation test in any language meant that Chinese, Japanese, and South Sea Islanders were easily excluded. This policy reflected many of the negative perceptions Australians had of Asians and of the Chinese in particular. The latter were suspected of rare diseases, sexual deviation, and inveterate gambling, and were also feared because of their huge population and relative proximity to Australia.[2]

1. *Cumberland Argus*, 28 July 1900, 4.
2. On Australian perceptions of, and dealings with, Asia during this whole period

Though these attitudes were not shared by everyone, their prevalence motivated Amy to talk up interesting aspects of Chinese people and culture whenever she had opportunity.

For her, Australians wanting to exclude foreigners was similar to the Boxers' antagonism towards Westerners in China. It made her more aware of how easy it was to be influenced by popular attitudes that had little to do with Christianity, as well as assume the superiority of Western values in all areas of life. Missionaries could as easily fall into this trap as well as others.[3] Generally, however, they understood that some aspects of culture were relative, for example how people ate, dressed, and socialized. They were also critical of some Western policies, such as the opium trade and purely money-making enterprises. In any case, living and working alongside poorer, rural Chinese helped make missionaries more sensitive to the difference between things that mattered and things that were simply cultural. On furlough, though, her main desire was to present the great need of missionary work in China. She did this in many different meetings around New South Wales—in churches, schools, public halls, YWCA meetings, and homes. Snapshots of these occasions were often reported in the newspapers.

> Miss Oxley, in Chinese dress, and exhibiting a number of Chinese curios and photographs, gave a very interesting and stimulating address on Chinese life and the missionary work in her district, explaining the rescue work among the blind and abandoned children . . . All the collecting cards for the building of a house for blind children . . . were taken up.[4]
>
> A most interesting address . . . dealt with three different features of the work—the educational, the evangelical and the medical. Miss Oxley expressed herself as thoroughly charmed with the work, despite its almost insuperable difficulties. One of the greatest of these, she explained, was that connected with the mastery which had to be gained over the peculiarities of the language . . . [She] exhibited during the evening a number of idols. Other curios (including the small shoes worn by the women of China) were shown to those present as were also photographs of the different schools conducted by the missionaries . . . During the evening, musical selections were rendered, and a collection

---

see the landmark study by Walker, *Anxious Nation*, and, most recently. Macklin, *Dragon and Kangaroo*.

3. On the extent to which missionaries did this, see Bays, *Christianity in China*, 71.

4. *Camden News*, 8 August 1901, 8.

was taken up. Miss Oxley is a ready and captivating speaker, and she treats her subject in a homely style.[5]

The meeting was held under the auspices of the Gleaner's Union. The Gleaners present appeared to take very deep interest in the charming account given by Miss Oxley of her experiences in the mission fields of China . . . A deeply interesting part of the evening's address was that referring more particularly to the efforts being made to uplift education and cheer the blind in China.[6]

Perhaps the most moving piece of writing from Amy's time on furlough was a poem written by a clergyman, W. H. H. Yarrington, who was also a lawyer, scholar, and recognized poet.[7] After hearing a public lecture Amy gave, he wrote a poem called *The Blind Chinese Boy*. Though, reflecting popular poetry of the time, somewhat sentimental, it captured aspects of what she had witnessed in China.

> I am a lonely Chinese Boy:
> I have no happiness or joy,
> But full of misery and pain
> I often cry and weep in vain,
> For I have none to love or care
> For all my sorrow, or to share
> My burden, and to give relief,
> And comfort in my childhood grief
>
> . . . My greatest grief is loss of sight:
> I never see the cheerful light,
> Or ne'er behold the lovely world,
> Whose beauty lies around and unfurled –
> The loveliness of flowers and trees,
> Whose bright leaves rustle in the breeze;
> I cannot see the light of love
> Which shines upon me from above
>
> . . . What do I hear—a loving word?
> Is it the singing of a bird?
> What is that note that sounds so sweet?
> A gentle hand, so soft and kind,
> Touching my eyelids dark and blind;

5. *Cumberland Argus*, 6 February 1901, 2.
6. *Cumberland Argus*, 13 February 1901, 2.
7. Yarrington, "Blind Chinese Boy." He was known for an award-winning poem on "Cook's Meditating on Australia's Future," written for the opening of the Great Hall in Sydney University and read at the unveiling of the Captain Cook Memorial in the city.

> As if they would my sight restore!
> The tears start from them more and more
> I feel a sense ne'er felt before—
>
> . . . They tell me that though I cannot see
> There yet is joy awaiting me:
> That one day, through God's loving grace
> I shall have sight and see the face
> Of Jesus Christ, the Savior dear
> Who suffered so much sorrow here
> . . . And then my pains will all be past
> And I shall dwell with him at last!

One of the highlights of Amy's time at home was catching up with her cousin and aunt at "Darriwill." Their strong interest in overseas mission meant that they were able to enter more deeply into her experiences in China, as well as appreciate the gifts—sterling silver letter openers engraved with Chinese characters, a beautifully embroidered tea cloth and tiny lotus slippers used for foot-binding—she brought from Foochow. With them, she didn't have to "be" the missionary; she could just be herself and talk about the lows as well as highs of what had happened to her. These weeks in Geelong brought refreshment and refocus for her return to China.

After more than a year in Australia, on 19 October 1901 there was a Valedictory Service for Amy at St Andrew's Cathedral in Sydney.[8] The next day she sailed on the *Eastern* for Foochow, along with fellow CMS missionary Minna Searle and several New Zealand recruits of CIM. On the voyage she wondered what lay ahead. Shortly before leaving, Amy learned that, alongside her work with the blind boys, she would replace the head nurse at the dispensary near the North Gate while she was on leave.[9] This was on the understanding that the seventeen blind boys from Deng Doi would be accommodated nearby.[10] She looked forward to this, and was grateful that while during her furlough she had raised enough money to build a new blind school.

---

8. *Brisbane Courier*, 21 October 1901, 5.

9. 77th Annual Report, NSW CMA, 1902, 13.

10. See the article by Amy Wilkinson for the Berrima Historical Society, in Welch, *Amy Oxley*, referred to earlier.

Meanwhile, the dispensary had just gained its first full-time doctor, George Wilkinson, from England. Though Amy was as yet unaware of it, he was to play an important part in her future. Until his arrival in early 1901, the only CMS medical missionary in Fukien was Dr. van Someren Taylor, who itinerated around the whole province and needed a colleague based permanently in Foochow. After falling ill on arrival, learning of his father's death shortly afterwards and an extended time in language study, George took charge of the dispensary, and planned to turn it into a hospital for all in the Old City. He had grown up in Sturton-le-Steeple, not far from Lincoln where his family farmed cattle. The village was chiefly known for being the birthplace of John Robinson, leader of the Pilgrim Fathers who sailed on the *Mayflower* to North America in the sixteenth century.

14 George Wilkinson (2nd row, 2nd from right) at Cambridge

After finishing school, George was offered a place at Emmanuel College, Cambridge with a view to ultimately studying medicine. He started in Michaelmas term, 1885, just a few months after the actions of several graduates of the university hit the headlines in national newspapers. Following a revival of interest in Christianity in Cambridge, these gifted young men scandalized the educated elite by offering themselves for missionary service in China. The best known of the so-called "Cambridge Seven" was C.T. Studd, the most celebrated cricketer in the country, who had recently played in the first Ashes Tests against Australia.[11] Intrigued by their story, George began to attend both mid-week meetings of the Cambridge Inter-Collegiate Christian Union (CICCU), and on Sundays Holy Trinity Anglican Church, the main student church. At the end of his first year, he went with other CICCU members to the Keswick Convention in the Lake District he heard Dr. Hudson Taylor, with whose CIM the Cambridge Seven had volunteered. This experience gave George a growing interest in overseas mission, perhaps in China.[12] This severely disappointed his parents' hopes that he would take up a profession at home.

After graduating with a B.A. in 1888, George began an internship with the Bolton Infirmary in London, working among the inner-city poor. Over the next few years, he continued his training, gaining a Social Apothecary Licentiate in London in 1891, Bachelor of Medicine and Surgery the following year, and a Master of Arts in 1893. In a short time, he became house surgeon at the Middlesex Hospital and then director of the Islington Medical Mission in the working-class East End of London. These positions were good preparation for China to which he felt increasingly called. On 7 February 1899, George applied to CMS and was accepted for Foochow. During the months before he left, he undertook some theological and cross-cultural study at the nearby CMS Training College in Islington.

Shortly after her arrival in Foochow towards the end of November 1901, Amy rented a building on Nantai Island as a temporary location for the Blind School, and arranged for the seventeen blind boys from Lieng Kong to join her. Sadly, two of the them unexpectedly died, and she had difficulty finding suitable blind teachers to assist in the work. Such challenges led her to write: "Why God has given me this work to do I know not, the very last kind of work I would choose but I am perfectly certain He has given it to me to do and I really do want to do it joyfully."[13] She was, however, encouraged by to the provision of a larger rented property in Hualin Lane that was closer to the dispensary.

During the summer, Foochow, which in hot months was vulnerable to plague, suffered a major epidemic followed by an outbreak of cholera. This resulted in thirteen hundred coffins being carried out of the city in one day. Dr. Wilkinson, Amy, and the Chinese nursing team were kept extremely busy. The strain on medical facilities hastened George's plans to open a small men's ward, add a new women's ward, and set up an operating room.

---

11. See Grubb, *C. T. Studd* and on the group, Pollock, *Cambridge Seven*.

12. On the nature of the movement's piety and its influence on mission, see Banks, "Keswick Movement," *Lucas*, March 2017, 48–72.

13. See NSW CMA Report, 1902, 12–13 and NSW CMA Report, 1903, 11.

Surprises of the Heart (1901–1906)

15 The Soul-Lighted School with Bible motto above entrance

He also offered his construction workers to help Amy build her new Blind School on land purchased between the hospital and the northern wall of the Old City. Wanting her school to reflect Chinese rather than Western architectural styles, she insisted it have an attractive, curved, pagoda-style roof. The whole building was designed as a place for blind boys to live, learn, and work. She was able to employ a matron, a committed Christian experienced in working with children.

Over the years Amy had been working with the blind, a picture kept coming into her mind of heaven as a place where everything would be fully restored, one in which crying, illness, and pain would be no more. She often talked to the boys about this. In naming the new school, she chose 靈 *Ling* (Spiritual) 光 *Guong* (Light) 盲 *Mang* (Blind) 學 *Hok* (Study) 校 *Hau* (School)—in spoken English, "The Soul-Lighted School."[14] Inscribed above its entrance were the words "They Shall See His Face"—a quote from Revelation 22:4, which continues "and His name shall be on their foreheads."[15]

---

14. Letter to Margaret Griffiths, 18 January 1902.
15. See the photo and text in Roberts, *Photography in China*, 48–50.

Amy, like many single female missionaries at the time, was so focused on her calling that she did not expect to marry. This was even less likely in a province where there were so few male missionaries, most of whom were married.[16] Since there is no hint of a romantic relationship in any of her previous correspondence, presumably she had little experience in this area. Because of an all-or-nothing approach to her work, she possibly appeared too threatening for any potential suitors. Amy's growing relationship with George, however, was nurtured through their mutual work, as her personal correspondence to Isabel over the following year indicates.

> Today I have been busy with out and in patients at the Hospital and this evening have been busy with a baby of 7 months who has bronchitis. I really do not know <u>how</u> I am going to do School and Hospital work. Of course Dr Wilkinson will come and see any serious cases, but then I have to carry out all his orders.
>
> I find it very difficult to get letters written with 9 paid people in connection with the Hospital and Blind School . . . I am <u>very happy</u> indeed here, happier than I have ever been in spite of having so much to do. I will enclose a copy of Dr Wilkinson's house and you will see how the bow windows and roof look. It is very much like the place we planned.
>
> I now have something of great importance to tell you and dear Auntie, I am engaged to be married to Dr George Wilkinson, a man whom I have met at all times of the day and night in connection with the medical work for six months and as the days have gone by I have found out what a true and good man he is. A most considerate Christian, a thorough missionary, and a clever doctor, I can see how wonderfully God has been working out His Plan and Purpose, I will only have to move next door. I think I sent you a photo of the house . . . not thinking I would ever live there. He will help me with the Blind School and I trust I may be of some help to him in his medical work. Oh I am very happy about it and I feel sure mother and Aunt Lizzie will be very happy about it. He is not an honorary missionary, nor has he private means. His father is dead. Mother and sisters and several brothers in England, but none of them in sympathy with him. Do pray for him when you pray for me. I hope some day you will know him. He gives us such helpful Bible readings

---

16. As reflected in the CMA Annual Report, 1899, 372–76. By the mid-1890s, in a population of 20 million, there were only 16 Anglican missionaries in the province.

every fortnight ... I want to write heaps but there are so many I must write to about this.

I think the wedding will be middle of October. There is nothing to wait for any longer as it only seems like just going next door. We have been working together all these months and we hope to go on doing so. You will probably want to know what I am going to do about a trousseau etc. I am not going to have one, but am writing to Aunt Lizzie about a few things I must have. One is a wedding dress. I think white Persian lawn ... They say I must ask all my missionary friends but I don't want anything grand ... he is so good and true.[17]

In further letters she wrote:

The more I know George the more I see how fortunate I am. He has already been awfully nice and thoughtful about my friends out here and he looks upon friendship as a very sacred thing ... No, George does not have a large banking account or a long line of Ancestors but he is true and good and God is binding us together in the bonds of His own love ...

I am at Kuliang but only staying in this house for a week and then go to Minna Searle. I have not seen George for a week and he was to have come up this morning, but a letter came instead saying he felt he could not with a clear conscience leave the work until Thursday, so we must be patient. I would far rather put God and the work first and I am glad he would, for I know he is simply longing to come up.

I feel that you can understand so well what it means to be loved by a good man ... I know I spent weeks in prayer about the matter, but I am fully convinced it is of the Lord. It was so wonderful the way in which He took me into Foochow City and right to the very spot where I should see so much of Dr Wilkinson ... I never would have grown to care for Dr Wilkinson if I had not seem him day by day faithfully doing his work and so truly caring to win the people for Christ ... the photo I sent is a bad one, it is difficult to get a good one out here. He has shaved off his beard, he looks very much younger, he is 36 years old, and I am 35, so that is just right.

The wedding was fixed for 11am on 1 October at St John's Episcopal Church, Nantai Island, with Archdeacon Wolfe and Rev. Martin performing

---

17. Letters to Isabel Hope, 27 December 1901, 5 March 1902, 3 May 1902, 8 May 1902.

the ceremony. After a wedding breakfast at the Wolfe's, the couple were to leave on their honeymoon by houseboat to Kucheng.

> It is three weeks today to the wedding day. I am on [Nantai] Island at present seeing about the making of my wedding dress. I suppose I am very foolish but I cannot help thinking of the wedding of the girls [her sisters] and their trousseaus when Father was alive. The few things I have got I had to get myself and my dear boat, the proceeds of the sale of it is going to pay for what Aunt Eliza got in Sydney . . . [PRIVATE: I was really disappointed . . . She is a dear old thing but no taste. The Orange Blossom was one <u>common</u> spray, the black dress a thick flounced canvas which would suit Mother. In Foochow the missionaries sometimes ask each other out to Dinner in the evening and at Xmas and . . . one can wear a suitable frock . . . but alas a thick-old fashioned canvas! Then the dressing gown. I asked for a flannel and she sent something like hers with dreadful red satin instead and very coarse lace on the neck. Oh dear, and the price of the things, 11 pounds, for just those and nun's veiling, and vests, etc. . . . everything is so expensive . . . I thought I didn't care a pin about a trousseau but I would like to have a few new underclothes. We will be pretty cramped in a boat going upriver and it will be funny for a man to see my things, but he is such a dear fellow and so awfully nice about everything and he understands. Mrs Wolfe is so kind and going to ask the missionaries and give them tea and cake afterwards. There will be over 80 of course. Most of our own missionaries are up country but I am friends with all the Americans and they seemed to make up their minds to come, invite or no. The two bridesmaids, Minna Searle and Marta Barr, are to wear white and buttercup ribbons.[18]

---

18. Letters written to Isabel Hope 11 July, 3 August (2); to Margaret Griffiths, 3 August, and to Isabel Hope, 27 August 1902.

Surprises of the Heart (1901–1906)

16 St John's Church, Nantai, where Amy and George married

Amy and George spent the first part of their honeymoon on the island of Sharp Peak. Then they took a 250-mile tour of inland medical mission stations by sedan chairs, from Kucheng in the west to Deng Doi in the east, where Amy caught up with her earlier co-workers. Their marriage brought with it not only a change in Amy's personal status, but in her position with CMS. At that time, a female missionary who married had to formally resign from the organization, stressing that it retained "a lively interest in her work," and continued to include reports from her in its publications.[19] George, however, always regarded her as a partner in their missionary work. For her, an advantage was that she could now decide without any reference to CMS where to direct her energies. Once the head nurse returned from her furlough, Amy could resume full-time work in the Blind School and travel on its behalf whenever and wherever she wished. Yet, publicly, no longer being referred to by her first name or her Oxley surname, but as Mrs Wilkinson, was an ongoing struggle.

---

19. George Wilkinson, Extracts from Annual Reports 1902–1908, CMS, 6 December 1902, 621.

On returning from their honeymoon, Amy and George were involved with preparations for the official opening of both the Hospital and new Blind School on Monday 1 December 1902. Those invited were local civic dignitaries, including the Chinese viceroy and British consul; representatives of missionary societies; CMS colleagues and local Christians; staff from other hospitals; and teachers and pupils from the Blind Boys School. There was an impressive fireworks display, which for the Chinese always heralded something important. In the dedication service, addresses were given by Bishop Hoare from Hong Kong, Archdeacon Wolfe, and George himself. Musical items were provided by the Blind School.

The school's new facilities gave Amy the opportunity to further develop her vision for educating the blind. During her recent furlough she had visited the Sydney Industrial Blind Institution—precursor of the Royal Blind Society—whose commitment to the whole person, and helping the blind become self-supporting, had enlarged her outlook. Up till now, her work with the blind boys had been largely instinctive, feeling her way rather than implementing a program. Now she had a clearer template and outcomes for what she wanted to achieve based on the Sydney Institution's motto of "Teaching Independence Through Industry."[20] Her more picturesque Chinese equivalent of this was "Feed your Mouth with your Hands." Amy now saw the school as a safe space enabling students to become well-rounded and self-sufficient adults, training them for specific occupations and finding placements for them in the workforce. For her, it also involved seeing the boys as made in the image of God, developing their spiritual growth and character, and having a definite purpose in his world.

Amy organized the school into kindergarten, junior primary and senior primary departments. In the kindergarten, activities were primarily focused around play. In the junior school, students learned their national language, abacus, singing, and Christian beliefs. In the senior school, they also studied history, geography, English, writing, and music.[21] As one would expect in a Chinese setting, relationships between students and teachers were respectful but tempered by a loving, family atmosphere. Amy rejected

---

20. In its later *The Sydney Industrial Blind Institution Newsletter*, 18 November 1905, 6, this acknowledged the "well-known Sydney girl" Amy Wilkinson for the work of her Blind School in an illustrated article wishing it "every success" and expressing confidence in its being "warmly supported in the future by the charitable community of this country."

21. *Fu Zhou Shi Mang Xiao*, 5.

the title "Principal" and insisted she be called instead "Auntie Teacher," a term that endeared her to the students.

After their morning studies, afternoons were given over to various kinds of work and play.

> This afternoon I sat down for some time and watched them; one boy was making a bamboo hen-coop, and I really marveled at the quickness with which he twisted the bamboo in and out; two boys were making bamboo blinds, one of them singing hymns the whole time; three boys were making rope, each knowing his part—three working as one; three boys were making basket-lids, and I can hear them chattering away all the time; one boy was making string; seven very small boys making twisted string, and I was surprised suddenly to hear [one] six year old singing, "Hark! the herald angels sing" really very correctly. One boy was splitting bamboos, and another was here, there, and everywhere—"little Quicksilver" I call him, as it is difficult to get him to sit still for five minutes. Then I pass through to the school room, and the hum of voices soon told me that no one was wasting his time there.[22]

Amy saw play as developing the boys' gross motor skills. Traditionally, Chinese children were often restrained so they would not harm themselves. The school playground now gave them a large and secure area for organized games, such as seesaw, tug of war, sung exercises like Hokey Pokey or Oranges and Lemons, climbing high and low bars, flag drills, and races. There was also opportunity for unstructured activities during the boys' free time. All these forms of play were used to develop posture, agility, cooperation, and confidence.

---

22. From the slightly later NSW CMA Annual Report, 1904–5, 6.

17 Students on exercise equipment

18 Older student serving in Hospital

As the blind can develop a heightening of other senses, such as hearing, music education was an important part of the school's curriculum. This strategy built on the Chinese tradition of the blind becoming traveling musicians. As much s possible, therefore, Amy incorporated singing, reading music, and playing keyboard instruments, such as the accordion and organ, into instruction. When it was possible, she enjoyed accompanying a choir on the harmonium. Already known for her skill in playing a tin whistle, people at home who knew her were "therefore not astonished to see in the CMA publication a picture of a drum-and-penny-whistle band, composed of boys from the blind school."[23]

Drawing on her own early experience as a pupil-teacher, Amy realized she could call on senior boys in the school to assist newer ones in learning Braille—not only teaching them to read but helping them experience something of what they were reading. They could also assist other boys to gain work and play skills. A few of the older boys even began to undertake pastoral work among patients in the hospital next door.

Amy's first-ever student, Ling Kai, was an outstanding example of this. Despite some occasional lapses in behavior, the worst of which was experimenting with opium, he had continued to make progress—educationally, vocationally, and spiritually. After helping to translate most of the New Testament into Braille, in 1903 he became a "missionary" teacher and began work among the blind in one of the inland provincial cities (whose dialect Amy also helped to translate into Braille). As this was a paid position, Ling Kai no longer required financial support (which until then had come from her cousin Isabel), and embodied the school's goal of making its students financially self-sufficient. When, two years later, a school for blind girls was finally opened on Nantai Island, Amy taught Braille to its first principal, Emilie Stevens from Tasmania, and Ling Kai assisted as a teacher.[24]

Apart from the occasional illness during this time, the Wilkinson's suffered a serious personal setback. In the summer of 1903, Amy wrote to her friend, Margaret Griffiths, in England.

> Well I am getting stronger, but am feeling the heat, which has been rather greater than usual. Unfortunately I had a fall some weeks ago and that brought on a miscarriage, but I am thankful to say I have made a very good recovery, and I think the rest at Kuliang will quite set me up again.[25]

Overall, Amy was encouraged by the growing number of students voluntarily offering themselves for baptism and confirmation. Undergoing these public ceremonies was a huge step in Chinese culture because it was

---

23. Mrs. Wilkinson, cited in Extracts from Annual Reports, 1902–1906, CMS, 553, one of a few instances in which Amy was still treated as an official representative.

24. Stevens, *Daybreak*, April 1907, 25. On this institution, see "The Blind Girl's School, Nantai, Foochow," *India's Women and China's Daughters*, 1 September 1905, 196–97.

25. Welch, *Amy Oxley*, 5 June 1903.

viewed as a rejection of family and tradition. Student numbers were also increasing steadily—from sixteen in 1901 to thirty five in 1902, forty one in 1903, forty seven in 1904 then fifty five in 1905. Her early dream of having a school filled with at least 50 students had become a reality.

During these years, work at the hospital also continued to grow. On the medical side, the expanded out-patients department saw a steady growth in numbers, and there was now more room for longer-stay patients. Since George viewed his role as that of a teacher as well as practitioner, he opened a hostel to train three medical students. After recruiting a Chinese doctor, Dr. Ding, to assist him, a new dispensary was opened in another location in the city. Looking towards the future, George drew up plans for a new men's hospital, with fifty beds. The foundations were laid in mid-1904 and the buildings were completed the following year. This led to his first significant contact with high-ranking government officials and business people. By 1905, the hospital contained four large general wards and seven smaller ones, and outpatient attendance increased to ten thousand, many coming from a long distance.[26]

For George, the spiritual side of the hospital's work was equally important. He introduced a brief half-hour service on Mondays, at which he often spoke, and a Communion service on Friday evenings. At these gatherings, his medical staff and trained Bible-women shared their faith and gave patients copies of a gospel or other Christian literature. Some patients, both in hospital or after their discharge, decided to give up their household gods, publicly professed their new beliefs, and asked to be baptized.

Through this whole period, George and Amy were so busy with their respective responsibilities that they often struggled to find time together. For this reason, they decided to rent a holiday house in Kuliang. They found one in Ox Fort Road and escaped to it whenever they had opportunity. Even there, however, George was sometimes called to deal with an emergency back in the city. They also enjoyed opportunities to itinerate together through surrounding districts, as this gave them more time to just be with one another.

On 7 April 1905, Amy and George's daughter was born at Cha Cang Hospital, bringing them great joy. She was given two names that Amy held

---

26. These developments are documented in citations from Wilkinson, and Baldwin in Extracts from Annual Reports, 1902–1903, CMS, 1905, page unknown.

Surprises of the Heart (1901–1906)

dear—that of her beloved cousin Isabel and the Oxley family name. From the beginning, Isabel was not always well and had difficulty sleeping. As she grew into a toddler she was slight and sickly, and she often had to be comforted by her Chinese *amah* (nanny) or parents. Not long after her birth, CMS supporters read the following disturbing news.

> A great joy: a great sorrow: and a great deliverance fell to the lot of Dr George and Mrs Wilkinson in the last year—the birth of a little daughter, later on the sickness as it seemed to death . . . and then, soon after, the great joy of receiving back this precious child . . . from the hands of our great and loving Almighty Father.[27]

Whether Isabel had allergic reactions to the food or climate or something more serious we do not know. For George, this mystery illness increased his desire to deepen his study of tropical medicine and hygiene during their forthcoming furlough in England.

19 The Blind School and Hospital, c. 1905

In the meantime, a different medical challenge was claiming more of George's time and energy: the effects of opium addiction. Over the years, women had occasionally come to the dispensary, and then hospital, asking how they could persuade their husbands to give up the drug. A small number of addicts had also turned up, wanting to free themselves from it. These numbers were minuscule compared to the scale of the problem. Towards

27. NSW CMA Report, 1905–1906, 6; and 1906–1907, 9.

the end of 1905, George experimented with a new way of treating the addiction. This led to what one of George's helpers described as "a most unique work with opium smokers" in a village of around one thousand inhabitants in the district of Lieng Kong.

> Of late, the opium-smoking had increased at an alarming rate, and the price during the last five years has gone up 400 percent, the fields and houses are being sold, and the village was on the verge of going to pieces. Last December four opium-smokers had gone to the CMS Hospital at Foochow, and were there cured by Dr Wilkinson. One of the men, who also took opium, daily secreted part of his allowance of pills, and when he returned home cured his wife with them. The fame of Dr Wilkinson and his pills became so great that the village determined to invite him to cure their opium-smokers.
>
> The elders and head-men of the village prepared a feast, at which they considered what could be done, and through the Christians they approached Sophie Newton who forwarded the invitation, with the result that the Doctor began work with them on 2nd March.
>
> The men ranged in age from 20 to about 70 years; five being over 60 and several had smoked for over 30 years . . . The physical distress of these poor men during the first two weeks [of treatment] was terrible; tears streaming from their eyes, pain, vomiting, and almost every aching sickness a person could conceive, while the craving was almost excruciating up to the last day . . .
>
> Much prayer was offered on our behalf for this venture and from the first God was manifestly with us . . . Up till March there had been continuous rain but on that day the weather broke, and it remained fair until after the three weeks when continuous rain came on. This was indeed providential as in the large and very open hall it would have been impossible and risky to keep them in.[28]

This treatment involved George administering tablets spiced with morphine to help wean patients off opium. It was highly successful but required carefully calculated doses that minimized the chance of their becoming dependent on it. In the village, seventy-nine men and nine women were cured of their habit. While afterwards a few lapsed, who were then

---

28. White, "Opium Smokers," *Chinese Recorder and Missionary Journal*, vol. 37, 1906, 628–31. See further accounts by Wilkinson, Extracts from Annual Reports, 1902–1906, CMS, 410–411; *Straits Times*, 24 November 1906, p. 8; Reinders, *Borrowed Gods* 51.

either expelled from the village or conditionally allowed to stay, most managed to remain free from addiction. The success of this treatment had two important results. First, it linked overcoming the habit with the Christian faith, especially since previous efforts connected with ancestral religion had failed. In light of this, the village's plans to erect a temple were replaced by the decision to build a church. Second, word spread about the extraordinary change that had taken place and led to other villages asking for similar help. In one of these, thirty men and nine women were treated and to celebrate there was a large fireworks display.

> In the meantime, important developments were taking place in wider Chinese society. The longstanding imperial system in China was in decline, hastened by its endorsement of the failed Boxer Uprising. In the early 1900s, Dowager Empress Cixi had initiated some significant changes—for example, providing the basis for a constitutional monarchy, preparing reforms in education and medicine, and framing a decree to ban foot-binding—but these were too few and too late for many among China's elite. Moves towards more extensive reform were gathering force.

Around this time, George was presented with a lacquer board by wealthy officials in Foochow, honoring his hospital's work in the area and listing names of supporters in the city who donated beds.[29] Buoyed by the way both their institutions were gaining wider recognition in Foochow, early in 1907 Amy and George headed off, planning to go to England first and then Australia. This would enable them to meet and introduce Isabel to each other's families.

---

29. *Mercy and Truth*, 1 September 1907, 280–84.

4

A Travelling Sight and Sound Show (1907–1914)

ACCOMPANIED BY A YOUNG, partially-sighted Chinese boy, Ding, in late April the Wilkinson family went on furlough. During their nine months in London, they lived at the Bolton Infirmary in Islington, where George worked as senior head surgeon to assist with the cost of completing a three-month professional diploma at the prestigious London School of Tropical Medicine. This institution focused on equipping medical people to deal with health issues in tropical countries throughout the British Empire. Just a few years earlier, one of the school's greatest students had won the Nobel Prize for his work on malaria. To this day, it continues to provide leading-edge, interdisciplinary research in the area of global public health.[1]

Although missing her Blind School, for Amy seeing the sights and sounds of the "home country"—particularly Yorkshire from where the Oxley and Marsden families hailed—was like a dream come true. Getting to know George's family and friends was a little daunting, but it helped her to understand him better as well as introduce Isabel to her grandmother, aunts, and uncles. At the Annual Conference of the Medical Mission Association in London, George was one of the international speakers representing the four largest member societies.[2]

After six weeks at sea on the SS *Persia*, on 26 March 1908 the Wilkinsons and Ding next arrived in Melbourne. It was now George's turn to meet

---

1. See the London School of Hygiene and Tropical Medicine website at www.lshtmnc.uk.

2. *Mercy and Truth*, May 1907, 131.

Amy's family and friends, and introduce them to Isabel. They traveled first by train to Geelong, where they were greeted by the Hope family, and driven by horse and buggy to "Darriwill," which George had heard so much about from Amy. Being in the country again reminded him of his own farming roots. The visitors reveled in the quiet and peace of the Australian bush; opportunity for over two months to rest, read, walk, ride, and simply "be" a family—which was very difficult for them to do in China—restored their health and hearts.

20 Amy, George and Isabel relaxing at "Darriwill," 1908

After traveling by train to Sydney, George met Amy's aging mother and some of her brothers and sisters. In early June, he began his CMS deputation work there and in some regional New South Wales towns. In these talks, his focus on the challenges and prospects for the gospel in the "new China" was remarkably prophetic.

> The conservatism of centuries is passing away, and with it great and new problems for the Christian Church are emerging. Only a few years ago the old standards of education—wooden, lifeless, unkeyed to the life of the people and to national progress—obtained. Now the old systems are going by the board and Western ideas of education are prevailing, with great and wonderful possibilities for the Chinese people. The old superstitions are losing their hold, and unless the Christian Church rises to the occasion, a national lapse into atheism, with disastrous consequences, will result.[3]

George always emphasized the importance of medical missions in advancing the gospel in China. The traditional medical system and its remedies were notoriously inadequate. There was little understanding of anatomy or of the value of anesthetics. Surgical instruments were crude, and the simplest operations beyond Chinese capacity. By healing the sick and relieving suffering, patients were not only helped but opened to considering the christian messge and way of life.

On his return to Victoria, George spoke to christian students at Melbourne University. This brought back memories of his days in Cambridge, and how talks he heard by missionaries there had such an impact on him. Over the next few months he spoke to a variety of groups. His schedule in the *Church Missionary Society Gleaner* shows his movements.[4]

July 18–23	Ballarat Exhibition (at which the Australian prime minister Alfred Deakin also spoke)[5]
July 24–26	Daylesford
July 27	Men's Meeting, St Thomas' Essendon
July 28	Ladies' Meeting, St Mary's Caulfield
	7pm Nurses' Meeting, St Hilda's Missionary Training House
July 29	8pm Christ Church, St Kilda, Annual Meeting Gleaners' Union

Back in Sydney, dressed in Chinese costume, Amy gave her only reported talk in the form of a lantern lecture at Samuel Marsden's old church, St John's Parramatta. She mentioned that on her return to China Alice Kendall, relative of Australian poet Henry Kendall, would be assisting her

---

3. *Maitland Daily Mercury*, 2 June 1908, 3.
4. *Church Missionary Gleaner*, 30 June 1908, 1016.
5. *The Advertiser*, 20 July 1908, 6.

at the Blind School.⁶ For the Wilkinsons, the extended period on furlough provided an opportunity to gain perspective on their work and consider plans for the future. It also gave them the promise of a second child, though he would not arrive until they had returned to Foochow.

———

In the meantime, movements for large-scale reform in China were gaining momentum:⁷

- In *politics*, the dominant figure was Sun Yat Sen, a trained doctor and baptized Christian who had committed himself to turning China into a modern republic. Before the Boxer Uprising he had formulated his "Three People's Principles"—nationalism (freedom from imperialism), democracy (along Western lines), and quality of life (involving land redistribution). During 1907–1908, Sun helped fund and sponsor six different military uprisings in the south of the country. Though these failed, city authorities in Foochow, several of whom were now Christians, were sympathetic to his cause.⁸

- In *education*, the elite Confucian examination system was brought to an end and new government schools were established throughout the country, including in Fukien Province. However, these were limited in number and still primarily for boys. They did not touch the average city or poorer rural children the missionaries were reaching.

- In *health*, anti-opium societies were being formed to confiscate the drug and treat addicts. This took pace in Foochow and some of its nearby districts. Strongly supported by missionaries, these societies organized parades and demonstrations of up to ten thousand people, public burnings of the drug, and the closure of over three thousand dens in the capital alone. Many farmers also stopped growing the plant. To the missionaries' embarrassment, however, the British government refused Peking's demands to close down the opium trade, insisting that over the next decade it be reduced by only ten per year.

---

6. *Cumberland Argus*, 19 August 1908, 2.

7. On this period, see Hsu, *Rise of Modern China*, 452–64, and more specifically, Schiffrin, *Sun Yat Sen*.

8. Dunch, *Fuzhou Protestants*, 55, 65, 77–79, 82, 103, 155–65.

Arriving back in Foochow, assisted through her pregnancy by Alice Kendall, Amy resumed her work. On 9 June 1909 a healthy boy was born in Cha Cang Hospital. Deciding he would bear both of Amy's family names, their son was baptized Marsden Oxley Wilkinson. In the spring, blind boys came from other parts of the province, from Canton, with one even from Singapore. What traveling to the school involved for one newcomer from an inland village in Fukien, is vividly described in a little anthology of *Everyday Tales of China*.

> There came a day when Daik-ong was the centre of a group of hospital nurses and patients all saying good-bye as he set out on the long journey to Foochow. He thanked people for their kindness to him, trying hard not to cry, which was very difficult ... presents of cakes, oranges and money were stuffed into his pockets. The loadsman was ready with basket, waiting for the passenger, but before he would start, Daik-ong insisted on sharing his presents with his friends.
>
> At last he was settled in the basket. Tears were very near, but suddenly the doctor thrust a wonderful [soft toy] elephant into his arms, and with that to comfort him, the loadsman lifted the basket upend and started off in earnest on the way to school.
>
> Through the streets and out by the West Gate of the city of Funing and across the long, sandy plain, pat, pat went the straw shoes of the loadsman. Now and then there was a rest for a few minutes, and then on again, until about an hour the first rest-house was reached, and the loadsman sat down to drink tea and smoke a pipe. Then to his joy Daik-ong heard the voices of friends, and some of the foreigners who were also on their way to Foochow. At the second rest-house a picnic under a big tree was fun. There were cakes and tea, and fruit, and again Daik-ong's hand was stretched out with an orange to be shared with someone.
>
> On the way once more, and before long the sea ... It was a happy boy who played on the deck of the good ship ... During the night he was carried ... on board a steamer, but after some hours on the steamer, he landed once more ...
>
> Out in the street again, people turned to look at the strange sight of a blind boy skipping along with his hand clasped in that of a foreigner. An old woman, sitting on a door-stop with all sorts of things to sell, was a great attraction to the country boy and a mouse that ran along only cost him a farthing! At last a rickshaw was called, and with all his treasures Daik-ong was lifted up and travelled with the foreigner.

Then came questions. The first was addressed to the rickshaw coolie: "Rickshaw-man, where do you come from?" The man was very much amazed, and answered politely. When the rickshaw man rang his bell the reason had to be explained. "Are we quite safe in this?" he questioned. Buses and motors sounded different bells and horns, and Daik-ong decided that "Foochow is a city of bells."

Next day he travelled in a crowded bus, where strange people asked him many questions, and he answered as well as he could, for the other passengers spoke in good Foochow dialect, whereas Daik-ong had a country language of his own.

When he left the bus and got into a rickshaw with his missionary friend for the end of the journey he said: "I notice one thing about carriages. If you have to trust to men to draw them, they are very slow: but if you can just push them like my own motor, or like the big bus we were in just now, they can run very fast. But the bus has something inside it to make it go by itself. What is it?"

A few days later Daik-ong was playing with his new friends, blind boys like himself, in the School at Foochow.[9]

Now with two children of her own to care for, especially with Isabel still sickly and prone to fits, Amy hardly had time to come up for air. George was also busy, not just with his responsibilities in the hospital but in writing up some of his medical observations and taking up opportunities to treat opium addicts in local villages.

Soon after he got back, building on what he had learned from his diploma, George wrote a report to CMS about the main tropical diseases in Fukien. Cholera, which tended to appear each year, always led to many deaths and every so often it reached epidemic proportions. Smallpox was another regular problem. Liver disease and elephantiasis were also common. Malaria occurred less in the city, but more in country areas. Over the previous few years, dengue fever had also made its appearance.[10]

---

9. *Everyday Tales of China*, 44–47.

10. This was compiled mostly from George's own words as Chief Medical Officer in the province. See also, Harford, 'The Climate,' *Mercy and Truth*, 56–9.

21 George Wilkinson, working from home in the hospital compound c. 1909

George still found himself called upon to deal with opium addiction outside the hospital. We are fortunate to have his detailed description of one such case in the first half of 1909:

> The day is bright and sunny in the village of Dusung. As one walks down the main street, however, neither the scent nor the scene is inviting. Various ponds are being cleaned out, and the mud is lying thick on each side of the pathway ... The sonorous voice of the gong-beater proclaims, in the intervals of silence, that the day for giving up opium has arrived, and that those addicted to this habit are to repair to the temple set apart for this purpose.
>
> Towards the latter part of the afternoon men of wasted, dusky, and not infrequently of morose and forbidding expression may be seen wending their way to the temple, carrying bed-boards and other paraphernalia needed during their sojourn there. The temple has been loaned to God's servants for

a fortnight that it may be turned into a hospital for opium patients . . . and yet this is the village . . . where in the past years it was difficult to get a hearing for God's cause. The little church, formerly an idol temple, and the adjoining dispensary, by their quiet, regular working, have doubtless prepared the way for this present opportunity. And greater wonder still, the literary man who formerly offered the most determined opposition . . . is the mastermind of this movement and responsible for inviting the foreign doctor to come and help.

It was not till about 9.30am that seventy men had collected. The local catechist then offered prayer for God's blessing on the undertaking, and the first medicine round was proceeded with . . . The general arrangement of the temple occupied by the opium patients was fairly convenient for our purpose . . . the front theatre-like half and the back temple half . . . separated from one another by a sort of courtyard open to the sky . . . In the recesses are 3 main idols. In the center is the main idol of the village . . . shrouded from view by a sheet hinge in front . . . If the idol had had ears to hear, it might certainly have heard during these days many things to cause it disquiet, although our practice was not so much to talk against the idols as pouring out the positive side of God's love and mercy through Christ.

Our patients consisted of seventy eight men and five women. The men were accommodated in the temple and the women had quarters in the women's station class building . . . The average age of the men I find was forty five and of the women thirty seven . . . It is interesting to look down the list of occupations of the men. Most, as one might expect, are tillers of the soil, but there are in addition, traders, two schoolmasters, three cooks, three barbers, the village constable, a woolgatherer, a goatherd, a mason, an opium shopkeeper, three men of no occupation, and two men of leisure . . . Why they began taking opium is also of interest . . . forty-five began to take it for pleasure, while the rest of the men and women for ailments, real or imaginary, of one kind or another. With regard to the length of time that opium had been taken, I find that the average term works out at about fourteen years in the case of the men and seven in that of the women . . .

With regard to the medicines used—they were mostly in the form of pills or tablets, containing as their most powerful ingredient opium or morphia combined with tonics and other substitutes. Our practice was to give them quantities graduated according to the amount previously eaten or smoked, for three or four days, and then gradually decrease the amount till the tonic was being taken. The medicines were always given under the most careful supervision . . .

Among other qualifications, some knowledge of human nature is needed. One patient needs to be commiserated, another needs to be joked with, while a third needs to be sat upon unmercifully. There is always, too, the patient who, whatever you give him, is always "like Oliver, asking for more."

We attempt to make an impression upon the moral and spiritual nature of these men in three ways: (i) by preaching, (ii) lantern lectures, (iii) the distribution of literature. The preaching was done at [non-compulsory] regular morning and evening services before the medicines were given round. We had altogether 4 lantern lectures in the temple when . . . quite a crowd of village people assembled . . . With regard to the literature, we gave each man to begin with a sheet containing on one side the Lord's Prayer, Ten Commandments, Creed and the Golden Rule, and on the other two hymns, viz., 'Jesus loves me' and 'There is a happy land.' Copies of St John's Gospel, attractively got up and illustrated . . . were freely distributed.[11]

After Chinese New Year 1910, Amy was approached by government officials in Fukien to consider displaying the work of the Blind School at the international Nanking Exhibition to be held in May. This was a tremendous honor and quite rare for an institution working with the disabled. It was China's first official world fair and was designed to showcase the country's growing agricultural, economic, technological, and cultural development. Occupying an area of 140 hectares, with buildings for various provinces, including Fukien, it provided displays of farm machinery, industrial crafts, transportation, education, health, and the arts. On display over the six-month period were more than one million commercial items. The importance of this event was summed up in the following way:

> The Nanking Exhibition drew extensive attention to people throughout the Chinese Society and attracted many high-profile merchants, scholars and Government officials to attend. There

---

11. Wilkinson, "The Loan of an Idol Temple, *Mercy and Truth*, 333–41. In his next official report, he noted that there had been a noticeable increase in spiritual response by patients, including "inveterate opium smokers" (Wilkinson, Annual Report, July 1910, 245).

were large delegations from Japan, the United States, Germany, and residents from Southeast Asia. It is estimated that over 300,000 people visited. Trades during the Exhibition were worth tens of millions of dollars. At the time, people considered it a great event in 5000 years of Chinese history.[12]

In the summer, a well-known figure in Foochow, Captain Wong, undertook to pay and care for the whole trip. Ling Kai and four other blind boys representing the province travelled to Nanking. This opened up the opportunity for Amy to present the school on the national stage of educational and industrial innovation.

> One boy [Ling Kai] obtained the White Button, which means a literary degree: others received a gold medal and certificates from the Viceroy of Foochow and from the official of the Nanking Exhibition. The boy who gained [it] is very bright and clever. He has written out all the New Testament in Braille . . . he is very musical and can speak . . . a fair amount of English. The other boys who have received the gold medals and certificates are also bright lads and will, we hope, be of great help in the future development of the School . . . The certificates are beautifully harmonized and attractive . . . These were presented by the Vice-President of the Board of Industry . . . Mrs Wilkinson, the founder of the Blind School in Foochow city has taught diligently and carefully the Blind boys to learn their lessons and to make articles. The School owes it success to the great and liberal help of Mrs Wilkinson.[13]

The recognition gained through the Nanking Exhibition opened up many more opportunities for the school, and especially for the Blind Boys Band. It was increasingly called upon to play at civic, church, and interdenominational functions. Invitations came from all over the province, even as far away as Shanghai. Amy provides an insight into what was involved in travelling with the boys to such places.

> There is great excitement in the blind school compound. Twelve blind boys from the school have been invited by the Chinese members of the YMCA to take their band up to Inghok for the

---

12. "An Overview of the Chinese Expositions During The Late Qing Dynasty—An Article Celebrating China's First Ever World Expo", Chinese Medal blogsite, www.chinesemedalblog.com, viewed July 2016.

13. As reported in the *Church Missionary Gleaner*, 1 October 1912, 170. Amy's more modest account of the event may be found in the *CMS Home Gazette*, November 1913, 343.

annual meeting. Bed quilts are folded up; baskets are packed with soap, facecloth, toothbrush, comb, oil for the hair, and extra clothes in case it is cold. The band instruments—not forgetting the organ, the kettle-drum, and the drum—are got ready; and all have to be made into loads, each weighing not more than 40 lb., so that a coolie can carry two loads, one on each end of a bamboo pole put across his shoulder.

Bang bang! at the compound door, and in come the sedan chairs with twenty-four chair coolies, each talking at the top of his voice and running about trying to grab hold of the smallest and lightest boy to carry. Poor Dai Ming, the cornet boy, is always last. He has grown so tall, but he smiles and speaks nicely, and in the end he is seated.

The next excitement is getting on board the boat. What a job it is to get comfortably seated, packed as tight as sardines in a box! But oh! the fun of it all. Off we start, and before very long we are hungry, so the cook prepares the rice in one pot and fries the pork and vegetables in boiling oil in the other. The smell of it makes your mouth water, and how delicious it is.

The night comes on. Quilts are unpacked, and preparations made for bed. But first we sing some hymns. On either side is the beautiful river; above thousands of stars shine in the clear sky. Not far off is a village, and you can hear "Knock, knock, knock." Someone is sick, and the Buddhist priest has been sent for to repeat prayers to the Buddha and is calling upon the idols for help. But these boys have souls lighted from on high, and they sing hymn after hymn, praising the one true God, and it is beautiful to hear their voices—bass, tenor, baritone—sing; "Crown Him, crown Him, crown Him, crown Him Lord of all." We read the story of Jesus walking on the water and Peter crying: "Lord, save me!"

At dawn we awake to find that we are getting near the rapids. Out jump the crew, leaving open the steersman holding on to his long oar. Men, women, boys, girls are waiting on the shore for a job, and soon they are all pulling the long towing boat with all their strength, sometimes with hands on the ground as well as feet. At last we have ascended the rapids. It is thrilling! If the rope broke the boat would be tossed back into the rushing waters and smashed to pieces on the rocks.

All day long, on either side, as we go up the river, are glorious wooden hills covered with dark green fir trees, light green feathery bamboos, scarlet and most beautiful colored-leaved trees, for it is autumn. The sky is deep blue and the warm sun is shining. I see all these lovely things, but my band boys are blind;

not one thing can they see. But there is never a word of complaint; they talk and sing and joke and tell stories. Why? Because they can say: "I am so glad that Jesus loves me, even me!"

22 Amy and Band on tour, c. 1909

Such a welcome we get in Inghok! Firecrackers by the thousand are let off and dozens of boys are each anxious to have the honor of leading about a blind band boy. The inhabitants look and look and wonder, and the excitement is great when the band begins to play.

One, two, three, four, beats on the big drum, and a burst of sound, 'Onward Christian Soldiers'. Soon the hundreds assembled to hear are catching the rhythm of the music and want the band to play on and on. But the literary men are longing to see and hear the boys read the Chinese classics, and then to write. To the scholars the Braille are 'magic dots'. They wonder why the 'foreign child' troubles to teach these things to blind boys, and we say; 'The one true God, the heavenly Father, has sent us', He is Love.[14]

In the midst of the school's success, in September 1910 came the sad news that Amy's mother Harriet had died suddenly. She was buried next to her husband John Norton in the family plot at Cobbitty. In her grieving, Amy was grateful that she had been able to introduce George and Isabel to her in Sydney and enjoy the time they had spent together in aunt Eliza's home.

14. *Eastward Ho*, May 1922, 51–53.

George saw the fruit of much patient effort in 1910. The opening of the long-awaited new outpatients building on 9 October was a "red-letter day." Attenders included the vice-president of the Provincial Assembly, representatives from the foreign settlement, doctors, and staff. In the lead-up time to the ceremony, some boys from the Blind School played a variety of English, Scottish, and Irish airs on the violin, cornet, and organ. After a hymn and a reading, the bishop and the American consul gave addresses on the importance of medical missionary work in China.[15]

A second major development for George that year was final preparations for the founding of the Medical Union College, a joint venture by Anglicans, Congregationalists and Methodists for the training of doctors. The official opening took place early in 1911 when Dr. van Someren Taylor was made its founding Principal. George continued to teach courses to the small but growing number of Chinese medical students.

July, Isabel's indifferent health took a decided turn for the worse and both Amy and George knew she needed treatment beyond what was available in China. Despite their busy schedules, they decided that Amy should take her to England to seek more specialized medical help. On arrival, CMS gave them great support and practical help. We do not know the outcome of the diagnosis and treatment but Isabel's condition eventually improved. While she was in England, Amy learned that a Triennial International Conference on the Blind had been held in Exeter shortly before she arrived. Disappointed at missing out on meeting with professionals on the leading edge of blind education from all over the world, she resolved to attend the next time it was held.

Back in China, during the last three months of 1911 events moved suddenly and quickly towards a political revolution.

> The revolution began with a minor uprising in military barracks in Wuching that unexpectedly opened the door to the fall of the Qing Dynasty. Hearing, from exile in America, that this rebellion against the imperial government was successful, Sun Yat Sen immediately returned to China. Meeting little resistance, the rebellion soon expanded to other centers in the country. In early November, revolutionaries in Foochow staged an uprising near the North Gate that resulted in the surrender of the Qing forces. A few days before Christmas, these regional insurrections culminated in the so-called Xinhai Revolution that led to the abdication of Puyi, the last emperor. Several days later, Sun Yat Sen was elected provisional president in Nanking.

15. Wilkinson, *Mercy and Truth*, January 1911, 15–17.

On 1 January 1912, China was enthusiastically declared a republic and the capital moved to Nanking.[16] While the authorities in Foochow supported the new republic, some soldiers of the old regime caused disturbances in the city. Though these threatened Christian institutions, supporters of the new republic were able to protect them. When news reached England about the uprisings in China it initially delayed Amy's return to Foochow, but by December she and Isabel were finally on their way home.

In March, two months after the declaration of the republic, Sun Yat Sen stood down in favor of Yuan Shikai, to whom he had promised the presidency if he brokered a surrender with the last Qing supporters. Shortly afterwards, Sun Yat Sen formed the Kuomintang, the National People's Party, as a step towards setting up a fully elected democratic system in China. However, elements of resistance to the republic remained. In Foochow, a bomb explosion threatened the life of a new civil governor, and counter-revolutionary plots continued to circulate. At one point the school was threatened, and a wealthy man in the city, not a Christian, offered to take all the boys into his home until the unrest was over.[17] Later in the year, Sun Yat Sen himself visited Foochow to thank supporters of the new republic there. Since George was now the supervisor of medical work in the city, he and Amy would have met the distinguished visitor at one of the gatherings in his honor.[18]

The new central government quickly set about instituting a number of key reforms. They founded new medical facilities, as well as new day and boarding schools for girls as well as boys. Amy's Blind School also continued to grow. By 1913 there were nearly eighty in the school. At home, Isabel's health had markedly improved. On Saturday 29 March, the Blind School had a red-letter day. A particular honor was the installation of its very first student, Ling Kai, to Mandarin status for his scholarly translations into Braille, and for his long-proven teaching abilities. Thirteen older boys also formally graduated from the school.[19] As one long-serving missionary wrote about the occasion,

16. On this series of events see Hsu, *Rise of Modern China*, 465–74.
17. *Mercy and Truth*, July/August 1912, 140.
18. On the strong growth of Christianity from the Boxer Rebellion to the Nationalist Revolution, see Bays, *New History*, 90–99.
19. *CMS Home Gazette*, November 1913, 343.

> Yesterday I attended the first graduating exercises of the Blind School under Mrs Wilkinson's care. They were of an unusually high quality ... one boy sang "Must I go empty-handed" [which was] very sweet. A quartet sang "Holy, Holy, Holy" in Chinese very well indeed. Two boys played the cornet, two the violin and they sang as a chorus "Hallelujah."[20]

A few weeks later, on 27 April, churches held a national Day of Prayer instituted by the new government. The decree ordered: "Let us all take part. Representatives of the provincial authorities are requested to attend the services which will be sincerely carried out by the entire Chinese and Christian forces of the nation." This took place exactly one hundred years after a Chinese imperial edict declaring that that the chief foreigner responsible for public preaching and private printing of books "to pervert the multitude" would be executed.[21]

Later that year, Amy received an invitation to address the next Triennial International Conference on the Blind in June 1914 at Westminster in London. The topic for this occasion was "The Exhibition of the Arts and Industries of the Blind." This was on an unprecedented scale, with a large and varied assortment of artifacts connected with blindness brought together in one place. Sighted and non-sighted delegates came from all around the world and included the blind American educator and activist, Helen Keller, as well as blind school educators from Australia.

Early in the conference, Amy spoke briefly about what was involved in adapting Braille to the Fukien dialect, illustrating this with a number of practical examples.[22] Her main address began by recounting the school's beginnings in Deng Doi and transfer to Foochow. She also traced the development from ambivalent responses among local people to high appreciation by national authorities at the Nanking Exhibition. This was followed by a tour of the school involving lantern slides. Her overall description of its premises, activities, schedule, and needs also foreshadowed something of her future plans:

---

20. From the Willard L. Beard collection, Yale Divinity School Library. library.yale.edu/divinitycontent/beard/Beard1913.pdf.

21. *Church Missionary Gleaner*, June 1913, 81–82.

22. Wilkinson, "School for Blind Boys."

A Travelling Sight and Sound Show (1907–1914)

23 Amy teaching balance on exercise equipment

24 Boys at the Blind School matting and weaving

A small gate in the thick mud wall admits us to the large, much-used playground. In front of us is a lovely banyan tree, beneath the shady branches of which the boys can sit and rest. We turn to the left and, walking through a covered verandah, come to the teachers' room, next to which is an airy schoolroom with one side completely open. Here we are greeted by a blind teacher, a lad whose intelligent face would single him out wherever you might meet him.

He is engaged in teaching a class of eight little boys, and one of these justifies the remark I made, that terrible indeed, sometimes, is the lot of the Chinese blind. This little fellow comes from Singapore, and, to avoid the cost of his rice, his own father tied him up in the jungle in the hope that some wild animal would relieve him of their parental responsibilities. On the same form sits another boy whose home was in the North-West Province. Being blind, and therefore useless, his father buried him alive, but the neighbors saved his life by digging him up again. The pale-faced boy near him was brought to the school a virtual skeleton—an open sore on his head and a bruise on his face. He was unable to speak or to sit up, but just lay moaning on the ground.

In the adjoining room, an airy apartment with one side open to the heavens, boys are learning to make bamboo blinds, baskets, etc. Five more frames for matting stand in an open verandah across the compound, and here the boys are of more advanced age. They stand up as we come in, and one man with a happy, intelligent face responds to our greeting of 'Peace.'

This man was brought to the school by his mother one cold, raw Christmas morning twelve years ago. 'I have no room for him,' I had to tell her, for my two tiny rooms were full. 'Oh, do take pity on him,' the woman urged, 'rice is so dear that his father says he will kill him if he stays at home eating it any longer.' Well, one does not look twelve years ahead in the face of such misery and—we managed somehow.

To return to the main building. Happy voices are singing as the busy fingers move quickly in making string. These are the little boys, and it is well to keep their hands occupied; they are employed in rolling straw and flax into string to be used later in the year for the straw mattresses on which they lie in winter. Others are making door mats from palm-tree fibre. Matting of some twenty different patterns, some with five colors woven into the design, is made here, and four matting frames are in constant use. The building is in native style, and the work carried on in the roomy verandahs that enclose a quadrangle.

Then we enter the dormitories—simple enough as regards bedding; the bed coverings show patchwork quilts made by kind friends in Australia and make the rooms look bright and cheery . . . to replace these in spring we have a few red blankets, as the native cotton- wool covering is too hot, and the boys are apt to throw them off in the night and catch cold in the chilly hours of the Eastern early morning . . .

Friends in England can always help us by sending out works in Braille—old magazines or books weeded out from the libraries will bring delight to the boys. One friend not only wrote out St Matthew's Gospel in Chinese in Braille, but at her own cost had it printed and sent to the boys. This gift encouraged us more than we can say, but I would just add this, that though we are missionaries we are not so narrow-minded as to think our boys should be fed on religious books alone. We want healthy work of all kinds that will widen their ideas and teach them something of what is going on in the world outside. Further, we find it difficult to get paper suitable for Braille writing, the carriage from England costing more than the paper itself, so that we often have to use up old newspapers for this purpose.

Now, leaving the schoolroom, we cross an open space at the sides of which are my study and the matron's room. And here a door leads us to the drill ground; the small boys do dumb-bell exercise every day, and the older boys are instructed in soldier drill.

In the large school we have a very good organ, and a very useful 'baby' organ. The boys are uncommonly musical for Chinese and play and sing in parts quite correctly. One plays the organ, another the violin, another the cornet, and so on; but we are very hard up for musical instruments, and if anyone has such a possession that is unwanted we should indeed appreciate the gift.

The boys assemble in the large school at 6 a.m., when prayers are said. At 7.30 a.m. an address is given by one of the pupil-teachers, followed by lessons, work, meals and play till 9 p.m., then the 'Last Post' is sounded, lights are put out and silence reigns.

The dining-room is next to the schoolroom, and is sparsely furnished with the typical Chinese wooden tables and benches, chopsticks and bowls forming the simple table equipment. The boys have three meals a day, consisting of rice, with fish, vegetables, etc.

Domestic work occupies a little of the boys' energies. On one side of the school buildings is a drying ground, and here, spread out on bamboo poles, some 250 garments may be seen every week—we occasionally receive a present of soap, and it is always most acceptable . . .

At the far corner of the drying ground is a small isolation ward for the reception of cases of infectious disease, especially small-pox and the like. On the other side of the school is a level piece of ground, where from end to end seven telegraph wires are stretched on posts some three feet high, the wires being a couple of feet apart. This is a device to exercise the little boys. Grasping a swivel in one hand, seven boys at a time can run from one end to the other of the playground as fast as they like in the comfortable knowledge that the way is clear and that there is nothing to stumble against. When boys first come to the school they usually creep and fumble around, but they quickly develop, and I think this running exercise gives them confidence quicker than anything else would. Playthings we sadly need for the younger ones—play is so good for them in every way—but we have little money to spend in this direction.

Beyond the playground is a garden. The poor little lads quite appreciate the flower's sweet scent, even if they have to rely upon the eyes of others for a description of their beauty.

What is to become of these quickly-growing boys when they arrive at manhood worries them as well as us. We are earnestly seeking the wherewithal to pay for the building of an industrial home on a piece of land, which is already walled in and in our possession. The idea is that a boy who has passed at least eight years of his life in the school and has obtained the certificate should be drafted into the industrial home, earn his own living and at the same time continue to study in the evenings. For some of the more promising boys there are other prospects—teachers, preachers and organists, but the majority must gain a livelihood in mat making or in working bamboo.[23]

In late July, Amy was one of three main speakers at the Saturday morning missionary meeting of the Keswick Convention in the Lake District.[24] Since the Keswick movement had contributed so much to her and George's spiritual journeys, addressing it was a great privilege. Scarcely was this over when external events took a momentous and unpredictable course. The world was at war in one of the fiercest and deadliest conflicts in history. What would this mean for missionary work in China? What would it mean for her work among the blind?

---

23. Wilkinson, "School for Blind Boys."
24. *CMS Gazette*, 1 September 1914, 286.

5

The Order of the Golden Grain
(1915–1920)

THE ONSET OF WORLD War I affected the Wilkinson family's plans for the rest of their furlough. They had intended to sail "down under" to Australia in November, then to New Zealand so Amy could represent CMS at the Marsden Centenary Celebration over Christmas. However, the German navy, now the most powerful in the world, posed a threat to any overseas travel. For safety's sake, Amy and George felt they should cancel their travel arrangements.[1] With extra time in England, they had the opportunity to think about their long-term plans. To maintain and expand the school, Amy needed to explore more commercial outlets for the sale of its products. Along with England, this could be done in the United States which, so far, was unaffected by the war.

Within a few weeks, Amy received a letter from the officials who had organized the Nanking Exhibition, asking if her school could supply items for the International Exposition in San Diego opening on New Year's Day 1915.[2] She arranged for her colleagues in Foochow to send a sample collection of woven bamboo, plaited ropes, and seagrass twine for making fine homewares, as well as prototypes of mats and chairs for exhibition. Impressed by the craftsmanship of the materials, the school was presented

---

1. This news was strongly regretted by the organizers of the Centenary and family members in Australia were naturally disappointed. See the *Maitland Mercury*, 7 December 1914, 3.

2. Ma and Ai, *World. Exposition*, 4; and *Daily Mercury*, 7 December 1914, 3.

with two silver medals, but unfortunately Amy's hopes for contracts from manufacturers were short-circuited when the United States joined the war.

As the fighting continued, bogged down in the trenches on the Western Front, Amy and George had to consider when and how to return to China. The bigger issue, however, was the education of their children. Most missionaries at that time organized their children's schooling in their home country. This was partly because the quality of education was better, it was provided for girls as well as boys, and there was support from relatives during the holidays. For these reasons, Amy and George decided it would best for the children to remain in England. When they broached this matter with the wider family, George's mother and his unmarried siblings, Jane and Horace, offered to look after them for the next five years.

After settling the children into school and sharing some good family times, on 23 January 1916 Amy and George boarded the S.S. *Mongolian*, a converted cargo ship recently repaired after damage by torpedoes from a German submarine.[3]

25 Amy and George, with Marsden and Isabel, in London, 1915

3. See the Atlantic Transport Line website at http://www.atlantictransportline.us/content/45Mongolia.htm, though by the time Amy sailed on the ship it was operated by the Pacific Steamship Company.

On reaching Foochow, they began to experience firsthand the wider changes taking place in China. Modern forms of lighting, transport, and communication were appearing, together with a more tolerant official attitude to Christianity.[4] Yuan Shikai, President of the Republic, had shown himself sympathetic to missionary work and even arranged a generous annual donation to the Blind School.[5] However, under his rule, the country began to move away from becoming a constitutional democracy towards the restoration of a dynastic system. Indeed, for three months, Yuan Shikai took over full control of the nation and proclaimed himself Emperor. A notable event during this time was the official ending of the opium trade on 1 May 1916. All remaining stocks were burnt and celebrations were held throughout the country, including Foochow. After Yuan Shikai suddenly died in July, civil war broke out in northern China, and Sun Yat Sen returned to take control of the Kuomintang government in the south. Though he strongly advocated the reunification of the country, it began to fragment into areas controlled by military leaders or "warlords."

At the same time, Cha Cang Hospital received some substantial gifts from officials in Foochow. In response to the hospital's help in caring for sick soldiers, the city's military commander presented certificates to graduating nurses, and its civilian governor gave the hospital a huge lacquer board on which was written:

> They Treat All Classes Of People
> Who Come To The Hospital Alike[6]

Over the next couple of years, the hospital, with a staff of ten (seven of whom were Chinese), and the evangelist Ling Kai from Amy's school, dealt with a higher than usual number of epidemics. The first was dengue fever, to which George fell victim.[7] As a result, he asked Ling Kai to write the annual letter to supporters about the spiritual side of the hospital's work.

---

4. Wilkinson, Letter, December 1917, 4 in the Wilkinson Collection.
5. See the comments of Rev. L. Lloyd in the *Church Missionary Gleaner*, 1915, 110.
6. *Mercy and Truth*, 1 September 1916, 202–4.
7. Wilkinson, "Facts from Foochow," December 1916, 1–4, in the Wilkinson Collection.

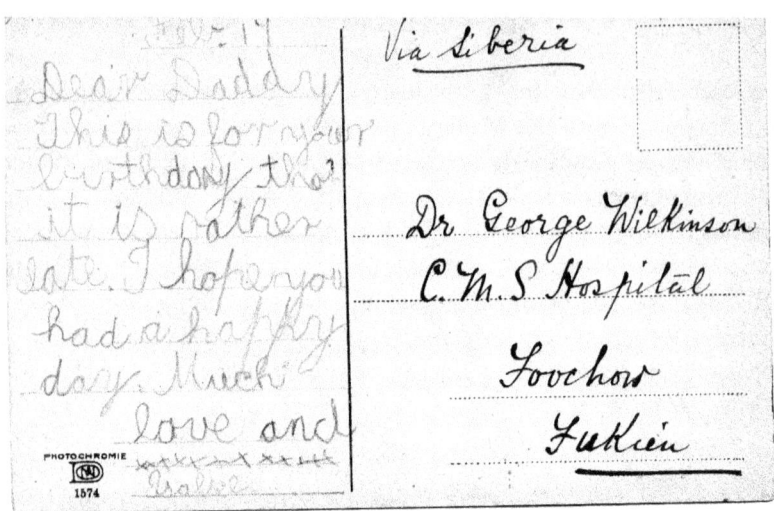

26 Postcard from Isabel to her father, pre-addressed by George

Nearly eight hundred patients stayed in the hospital last year. Some of the patients were very pleased to listen to God's Word, as we have been to their rooms to talk to them every day. We have given them the Gospel books to read and explained the story of Jesus to them. We have also taught them to learn the Lord's Prayer, the Ten Commandments, the Creed . . . We wish all the patients who come to the Hospital to hear God's Word . . . most come from other districts or other countries, very far away from the city here, so that it is difficult to tell how many patients believed in Jesus very year. But in the city we have seen that some of the patients have been to church the Sunday after they left the hospital. And . . . we have also heard from the catechists, who belong to the churches in the other districts, that they have found some patients who left the hospital here joining congregations in other districts.[8]

Missing Isabel and Marsden, George decided to write his annual Christmas letter to the hospital's child ex-patients. For the country children, he commented on the latest developments in the city—"wide level roads, electric light, telephones, public parks, rickshaws, horse-carriages, and an occasional motor."[9] Meanwhile, Amy received a copy of an interview she had given on furlough to a journalist from the American Foundation for

8. *Mercy and Truth*, 1 July 1916, 125.
9. Wilkinson, Letter, December 1917, 1–8.

the Blind. On the front cover of its highly respected international magazine, *Outlook for the Blind*, a photo of the "Foochow China School for Blind Boys" stared back at her.

> The illustration which we use for our frontispiece has been sent to us by Mrs George Wilkinson . . . who . . . deserves the approbation of workers for the blind throughout the world. Single-handed . . . she has solved for herself many of the most difficult problems connected with the education and training of the blind . . . Her splendid idea of adaptability and energy is shown by the fact that she discovered for herself that the blind boys could make the well known Chinese straw matting, samples of which she brought with her to London, and while there secured promises of orders from one of the best wholesale furnishing houses in England. The purchasing agent assures her that the quality of her blind boys' product was superior to that of similar material sent from the Orient. If the war had not intervened, Mrs Wilkinson would undoubtedly have had many orders for her boys.[10]

Receiving the magazine motivated Amy to begin writing a booklet to describe the growth, practices, and goals of the school. Drawing on her earlier reports and lectures, and adding photos, the result was *The Soul-Lighted School of Foochow*. Amy saw this as a tool to promote the Blind School and help secure its future.[11] Her account opens with a description of the school's beginnings in Deng Doi, her learning and translation of Braille into the Foochow dialect, as well as the introduction of trades into the boys' education. She then invites the reader to contrast these humble beginnings with the school as it exists today.

> It is situated at the north of Foochow, the provincial city of Fukien. The scenery is beautiful—a very fairyland of peach blossom in the spring—but alas! the boys cannot see its beauties. As you enter the compound, one of the first things to impress you is a white board hanging over the entrance gate, with four large black Chinese characters . . . 'The Soul-Lighted School'. Many Chinese look up at these characters, and ask: 'Why is this school called 'The Soul-Lighted School?' When told that every one of the ninety, or more, pupils are blind: 'Truly is that so?', they

---

10. *Outlook for the Blind* 10 (Spring 1917) 4, 42–44.
11. This finally appeared under that name and was published by CMS around 1920.

exclaim, and often walk up to the first boy and gaze into his eyes, and say: 'Truly it is so!'[12]

Asking her readers to imagine themselves as a typical Chinese visitor being shown round this school for the first time, she goes on to describe the varied programs for the range of her students.

> You walk into the drill ground and see some sixty boys marching to the stirring sound of the brass band playing, 'Onward Christian Soldiers'. Knowing that you are Chinese, the band will tactfully strike up a well-known tune, 'Mi-le-hua', and then the boys will sing a quartet in English and Chinese or play on the organ.
>
> After this you will be conducted to a classroom where you will find that the boys, though completely blind, can write or read any colloquial or classical sentence, using the ordinary English adapted to the 'Initial and Final' system. They can write English on a Blick Typewriter, and work with mathematical problems on the board made for the purpose.
>
> In the kindergarten you will see the little ones are taught to run by holding on to a swivel attached to a telegraph wire stretched between posts twenty yards apart. These small people will next entertain by walking on stilts, climbing swinging ladders and slippery poles, singing, marching, and playing games, all the time brimming over with fun and merriment.
>
> Suddenly a bugle strikes up. 'Come to the cookhouse door, boys' and these blind fellows rush across the compound to the dining-room. As they reach their allotted place, they sit down quietly, but at the word, 'Pray', they stand, cover their faces with their hands and reverently thank the heavenly Father for that day's bread. Being Confucianists, you are told the meaning of the prayer to the "One true God ad heavenly Father', and are much impressed . . . Before departing you ask 'Where does the money come from to feed and clothe and educate all these blind boys?' and are told that the work is one of faith, daily asking the heavenly Father for daily supplies. Then you take your leave, bowing courteously, and still saying: 'Wonderful, wonderful!'
>
> Yes, it is wonderful even to us to see the school with its ninety-five boys sent by the different missionary bodies working in the Fukien Province; or coming, as do some of them, even from Singapore. But to the Chinese, there is a greater wonder still. Confucianists, Taoists, and Buddhists do nothing for the blind; they leave them to die or beg or earn their living by

---

12. Wilkinson, *Soul-Lighted School*, 2–3.

fortune-telling. And when they see this school, they realise it is the outcome of the Christian religion, which is one of love.[13]

Amy then shifts the focus to the educational philosophy underlying the boys' work and study.

> It is interesting to note how a blind boy begins to learn. We will watch one of 8 years old: he has only been in the school a month, and is busy picking out strands of tangled flax one by one and holding them in his left hand... When he has learned to gather these strands of flax mechanically, he is seated next to a boy who is making string out of them by rolling and twisting them in his hands, and is taught how to do it himself! Both this kind of string and another, made of short strains of sea-grass, are used in the school—the flax for the outside of the matting and the sea-grass for binding rice-straw mattresses, of which we make hundreds in the autumn season. We can also sell any quantity of sea-grass string for tying up packets of tea, or for sending to Australia to be used in making fancy chairs; so the small boys are not wasting their time but begin at once to help in the school. From string-twisting, the boy goes into the bamboo department and there learns to plait bamboo, which has been cut into length about half an inch wide.
>
> Each boy works for half a day at learning a trade and for half a day at his books. At the end of eight years, he must be able to make a complete basket, or thread his matting frame, and make at least a foot and a half of matting in an hour. In addition to his trade, he will have leaned kindergarten action songs, singing, probably organ or orchestral music, reading, writing, and other subjects included in the lower primary course. Needless to say, he has daily instruction in the Bible and Prayer Book. If he can pass his examinations, he is given a certificate, and can become an industrial worker, and begin to earn money, living in the school, and paying for his food and clothes...
>
> If a boy wishes to become a preacher or teacher he leaves off working at his trade... and enters the higher primary department where he is trained to become a pupil-teacher. At present there are former pupils making a living for themselves; three are evangelists, one a teacher in a small school for the blind, one organist to an evangelistic band, and one assists in the C.M.S. Hospital, Hingwha.

---

13. Wilkinson, *Soul-Lighted School*, 4–6.

Next Amy writes about the benefits of what she calls "drills," activities that develop students' gross motor skills, spatial awareness and social interaction, which have:

> a beneficial effect upon these boys, many of which are very delicate when they come to us. It is delightful to see them learning to march quickly, and to go in and out of doors as if they were gifted with sight.
>
> The boys love football, but the playground is very inadequate, and when they kick the ball, it frequently goes into the street and is at once picked up, and carried off, never to be seen again. Tug-of-war, to say the least of it, is very exciting, so exciting that at time the rope is suddenly twisted round the veranda post by an over-energetic boy, and down comes the roof. Swinging ladders, climbing poles, see-saws, etc., are all in use, but so close together that one is afraid lest the boys should hurt each other.
>
> Then there are other games, e.g., the color game: a round board is divided into triangular sections, painted red, blue, green, white and yellow. Each section has two poles, with pegs for them of the same color as the section. The pegs are put out—the red peg into the red section, and so on—are placed into baskets which are about ten feet from the board, and the boys each pick out a peg and run to the board. The peg has a distinguishing feature on it, which the boy feels with his finger. They play the game very quickly, and people wonder how the blind boy can know the color.
>
> Then there is the Red Cross game, played by the lads in the kindergarten, and designed to help them understand something of what Red Cross flags, guns, and wooden horses, accompanied by a 'doctor and two nurses' is like . . . When the 'firing' begins, the little boys shout, and pretend to let off their guns, one or two fall down, and the Red Cross men come and carry off the wounded and bandage them . . .

The Order of the Golden Grain(1915–1920)

27 Red Cross drill at the school

In conclusion, Amy writes about a very distinctive feature of the school.

> Music and singing are a great joy to the majority of our boys, and to facilitate their learning, we have adopted the English Braille system for writing music. We began in a very simple way with a two-string Chinese violin, and found it possible to play a tune on these two strings, a penny whistle, a harmonium, and a Chinese drum. Later on we had a penny whistle band. Then we added a bugle to our stock, and a cornet. Learning to play upon the cornet made it easy for us to master other instruments when we got them. From time to time the band has visited other places, and acted, one may say, as an advertisement for the school. The audiences have been astonished, not only at the playing, but at the various other things the pupils can do. Our great hope is that many of these young lads as they grow up, may be 'called to the work of evangelists' and going into country districts, may perhaps start by teaching music and singing, and so gather the people round them to hear the good news of the Gospel.[14]

---

14. Wilkinson, *Soul-Lighted School*, 6–11.[JF]

28 The traveling Blind Boys Band

In the autumn of 1917, Amy organized concerts for the brass band in the regional centers of Amoy, Ningteh, Funing, Fuan and Lieng Kong, as well as Swatow and Canton in neighbouring provinces. Over a two-year period, it performed more than twenty times. Many school classes and wealthier Chinese attended the concerts, groups that Christian workers in the areas had found difficult to reach. In Fuan, officials presented Amy with a silver and enamel cup to commemorate the visit. On their trip to Lieng Kong, Amy and George took her brother Fred Oxley and his wife, who were visiting from Australia, to her old village of Deng Doi. Meanwhile, back in Foochow, she was delighted at the way students were taking the initiative in serving the wider community.

> The Blind School is responsible for a small Sunday School in the city, and blind boys teach in several others which have been started in neighboring villages. They also help with services at

the nearby CMS Men's Hospital . . . One senior boy has returned to Singapore where it is hoped that he will be of use as a teacher.[15]

On 14 August 1917, the Chinese government entered the war against Germany by sending 140,000 soldiers to join the Allies in France. This was largely a political move designed to strengthen the country's bargaining power against growing Japanese influence in the north Pacific. Japan had its eyes on part of the nearby Chinese province of Shandong that Germany currently dominated. For the Wilkinsons, this development reminded them afresh of their own relatives and friends who were fighting on the Western Front—young men like Amy's nephews John Oxley Norton and John Row, as well as George's brother, Horace, who had been helping to look after Isabel and Marsden.

In late November, Amy heard that her much-loved aunt Eliza had been paralyzed by a massive stroke. Two months later, when news of her death finally reached Foochow, Amy was comforted by the knowledge that one of her aunt's "old girls" from the Marsden Training Home, had sat on the edge of her bed and softly sung her into heaven.[16] A personal milestone for Amy herself took place on 13 January 1918, her fiftieth birthday. According to Chinese custom, it was the first birthday she could legitimately celebrate since her arrival. The occasion made her conscious of how much she would like to visit Australia again. Doing so would enable her to accept an invitation to attend the Oxley Family Centenary celebration in her home state in September. Since she had missed out on the Marsden Reunion in 1914, George encouraged her to make an extended visit.

Sailing into Sydney's magnificent harbor on a crisp day early in August was exciting. Amy was looking forward to staying with her sister, Beatrice, in the seaside suburb of Coogee. As well as connecting with supporters of the Blind School, she wanted to catch up with her family who were scattered throughout the state. First on her list was her childhood home, "Kirkham." Then, with Beattie, St Paul's Cobbitty to see her mother's and aunt Eliza's graves, especially as she had missed both their funerals. Walking around the cemetery brought back many memories of her Hassall grandparents, her father, and eldest sister and caused her to consider the cost of spending almost half her life away in China.

Amy's return to her homeland was greeted in *The Sydney Morning Herald* with an article and a photo of her school entitled "Teaching Blind Boys: A Missionary Starts with one Child and now has 95."[17] While she was

15. *Church Missionary Gleaner*, 2 July 1917, 71.
16. Welch, *Amy Oxley*, Appendix 2.
17. *Sydney Morning Herald*, 4 August 1918, 13.

in Sydney, her cousin Isabel travelled up from "Darriwill" to see her. It had been ten years since they last spent time together. There were so many stories to tell and memories to recall. When they said goodbye, little did either of them know this would be their last opportunity to see each other. After enjoying further time in Sydney, Amy and Beattie travelled by train to the sizable regional city of Wagga Wagga, where her brother Fred was the shire engineer. During a relaxed time there, she spoke twice at St John's Anglican Church, with the local newspaper highlighting the wider relevance of her work: "She had found that the blind were excellent teachers of the blind and in this connection suggested that returning blind Australian soldiers should be taught by the blind."[18]

The sisters then traveled north by train to the Oxley celebration in a larger regional center, Tamworth. Breaking their journey in Newcastle, the state's second main city, Amy gave an illustrated lecture in an interdenominational missionary exhibition, joining with missionaries from "various parts of the world to . . . bring stay-at-home people into touch with the ways of life of remote peoples."[19] Arriving in Tamworth, Amy and Beattie were met by other family members who were also guests of honor at the Centenary. The date chosen for the event was 2 September, the day John Oxley had discovered the river on which Tamworth was founded. The state's premier was present, along with six descendants of whom Amy was the most prominent. The event included multiple receptions, two public dinners, official ceremonies and a children's picnic. Its climax was the unveiling of the foundation stone for a monument to honor its discoverer.[20] As the Oxley family's representative, Amy "thanked the people of Tamworth for their wonderful hospitality . . . [and] whole-hearted friendship."[21] She then traveled down to the Southern Highlands to spend time with her sister, Mary Row, and visit places from her childhood in Bowral, the site of which had been donated by her father in 1859.

While Amy was away, George continued his work at the hospital and had a break in their holiday home in Kuliang where he was free to do what he enjoyed most.

> My delight is to dig and weed in the garden, to roam about and visit fern and orchid haunts, to listen to the music of the gorge and the soughing of the pines, to welcome the bird and animal visitors (a squirrel or a jay or a sparrow hawk or an owl as the

18. *Wagga Wagga Daily Advertiser*, 26 August 1918, 4.
19. *The Daily Sun*, 28 August 1918, 4.
20. *Sydney Morning Herald*, 5 September 1918, 3.
21. *The Tamworth Daily Observer*, 5 September 1918, 5.

case may be), to view the beauties of sunrise and sunset over the range upon range of hills and the river in the distance ... God seems to come near in the silences of the hills and there is a deep meaning in the Psalm that says: "I will lift mine eyes to the hills from which cometh my help' (Psalm 121:1).[22]

A sad event around this time was the death of Ling Kai's baby only a few months after he had lost his wife. As George writes:

> The poor fellow was frenzied with grief and it seemed for a time as if he would lose his reason but God's calm conquered and he was quite calm the next day when the small funeral took place up the hillside outside the North Gate.[23]

In addition to this tragedy, an outbreak of smallpox struck down fourteen boys in the Blind School. The school also had to be temporarily closed during some unrest in the city, but several wealthier citizens took in nearly thirty boys whose homes were too far away. "Some of these men are 'near to the Kingdom of God' and do Christ-like things but it is difficult for them to really identify with Christ."[24]

On the twentieth anniversary of the hospital's work, it was especially pleasing to see that the work "has now won an established position in this central city and indeed in a great deal of the northern part of the province as well."[25] This acceptance was despite limitations imposed by equipment, financial constraints, and treatments that some patients would not allow.

> Around this time there were noticeable contrasts between Chinese and Western influences in Foochow. Walking down its streets, you would see both ladies in European dresses and women with bound feet, shops selling up-to-date medicines and others traditional herbs, and motor cars alongside sedan chairs. On public occasions, you would sometimes encounter anti-Western and, indirectly, anti-Christian attitudes among students and intellectuals, sometimes erupting in demonstrations. These protests contributed to the growing nationalist feelings, violent student unrest

---

22. "A Summer in Foochow City," 1918, 6–7, in Wilkinson, Family Collection in the Cadbury Library at the University of Birmingham.

23. Wilkinson, "A Summer in Foochow City," 1918, 6–7, in Wilkinson, Family Collection in the Cadbury Library at the University of Birmingham.

24. Wilkinson, "A Summer in Foochow City," 1918, 5, in Wilkinson, Family Collection in the Cadbury Library at the University of Birmingham.

25. Wilkinson, Letter to Supporters, December 1919, 1, and for other information on the year's activities, 2–14 in the Wilkinson Collection. See also his article written the same year on "Abdominal Surgery," *China Medical Journal*, 1–6.

> and ultimately the birth of the Communist Party that were to mark the country in the following decade.

Amy's return to Foochow in late October 1918 was bittersweet. On reaching her school, she heard that around sixty of the boys had contracted the Spanish influenza virus that had infected millions of people worldwide. With the hospital nearby, however, medical intervention was able to prevent any dire consequences. When on 11 November the Armistice was signed, George and Amy arranged a thanksgiving celebration in the hospital compound. Doctors, nurses, medical students, and blind boys gathered around the flagpole flying both the British Union Jack and Australian Southern Cross, giving thanks to God for peace at last.

Within days of the Armistice, Amy was informed that during her time in Australia, Mr Hu, a Hanlin scholar, and Mr Guok, head of the Confucianists in Foochow, had invited sixty officials, literati, and headmasters in the city to a feast. The purpose was to petition to the president of the Republic to confer on Amy the "Order of the Golden Grain." This honor, the highest that could be conferred on a foreigner, had only been awarded once before to a Westerner.[26] Though she knew the process could take months or even years to complete, Amy was overwhelmed by this gesture

At her school, her main challenge was finding space for additional boys for whom there was no room. This was highlighted in the story of:

> an exceptionally bright, intelligent, and thoughtful boy of about 10 years of age. When he was brought to us, I had to say (as to over 30 other blind boys), "We cannot take you in, there is no room at the school." He answered pitifully: "Put me on the floor to sleep, put me anywhere, only let me come in." He wept bitterly when he thought he had to go home, which to him meant utter wretchedness. What could we do but squeeze him in? He did not know anything about God, had never heard of Him. Now he has been in the school about three weeks. The other day I was talking to him, and asked if he really loved the Lord Jesus. He

---

26. This was to Emily Hartwell of the American Board of Commissioners of Foreign Missions that year. She was recognized for her work in education, notably industrial schools and orphanages.

The Order of the Golden Grain (1915–1920)

said: "Yes, I do." I asked: "But why do you love Jesus?" He did not answer for a while. I sat in silence. Then he said: "He loves me."[27]

Towards the end of the band's two-year long visit outside Foochow, it performed in Hingwha for the opening of new Women's and Boys' Schools.

> Though the poor boys were thoroughly tired after their three days journey, they played splendidly for over an hour . . . The feast tables were soon deserted after the band struck up and all the crowd gathered round to watch the boys, who looked so smart in their blue uniforms and red bands worn over the shoulder, on which were the characters of the school.[28]

In Amoy and Swatow, many thousands of Chinese attended the performances, and gifts not only covered the overdraft but provided enough money to carry on the school's work for six months.

In preparation for the Wilkinsons' upcoming furlough, and with a view to the Blind School's future, Amy appointed a new principal, Rev E. M. Norton. He was a CMS missionary from England who already had several years' experience teaching at Trinity College in Foochow. His wife Edith, who had been a missionary in Japan, was an Australian from Tasmania. Meanwhile George arranged for his Chinese colleague, Dr Ding, to supervise the Cha Cang hospital while he was on furlough.

In July 1920, Amy received news that the request by the leaders in Foochow to honor her with the Order of the Golden Grain had been granted. *The Church Missionary Gleaner* highlighted the event on its front page:

> [It] was made a public occasion, and not only by the teachers and boys of the blind school; the streets of the city were decorated, and the Governor's band marched for miles displaying the official board which was to be presented. Altogether it was a gala day, and more than a thousand guests flocked to witness the formal presentation of the gold medal and the honorary boards, and to offer their own congratulations.
>
> The most important items on the programme were, of course, the presentations. There were boards from three Confucian bodies and two educational societies, from the Governor-General, the Mayor of the city, the chairman of the Chamber of Commerce, and others. There was a gold-medal from the Governor-General, and it was announced that a special Order of the Golden Grain was to be presented [on behalf of] the President. The last and most impressive of many speeches was by Mr Guok

27. *Church Missionary Gleaner*, 1 April 1920, 87.
28. *Church Missionary Gleaner*, 1 September 1919, 124.

[the Confucian leader] himself. The old man's gratitude for what had been done for these helpless boys struggled with a sense of shame that it had been left for a foreigner to do it.[29]

29 Amy's Order of the Golden Grain Medal

However grand the occasion was for Amy, her own children were never far from her mind. She asked Edith Norton, the wife of the new principal, and their son Teddy to write a description of the event for Isabel and Marsden. This was full of personal and colorful details.

> I do not need to tell you that Mrs. Wilkinson is a very wonderful lady. But you will be very pleased to hear that everyone in Foochow has just begun to realize it . . .
> I went to her house this morning at about 10.30 and the first thing I noticed was that flags were flying all down the main streets. This was in her honor! When I got to the house I found everything looking perfectly beautiful. The big gate was festooned with a thick arch of evergreen and flowers. Union Jacks and Stars and Stripes and the Chinese five colored flag were flying in conspicuous places. A great platform had been erected

---

29. *Church Missionary Gleaner*, 1 November 1920, 245.

in the garden with a large white awning over it to keep out the sun...

You know the tennis lawn. Well the platform was at the shady end under the trees, just below the little Summerhouse. Then up in terraces of the steep bank were chairs and forms, and at the bottom of the lawn were seats for the Chinese ladies...

The drawing room was for the officials and 'big men'—the dining room was for the less important men and the study for the ladies. So you see there was nowhere to have lunch at all. Where do you think we had it? Out in the garden under the trees, such a grand lunch too... Mrs Wilkinson looked awfully nice in a green silk coat with a lovely lace collar. She was quite nervous because she was to be the centre of attention, but all the same seemed perfectly calm and planned every little detail quite splendidly.

The doctor donned a cream suit for the occasion and was in great form. The day was simply beautiful: it could not possibly have been better. Lovely bright sunshine and not too hot. It made us all in a very smiling mood to start the afternoon.

I was in the ladies room receiving visitors from about one o'clock onwards [with] quite a number of Chinese girls and we all wore a red silk ribbon with our office written on it in black Chinese characters. The other folk were showing the ladies from the house to the garden and into their seats out there. Of course the men guests had their special receiving hosts too, quite a little army altogether was necessary.

Mrs Wilkinson's duty was to sit still and do nothing and a very hard one she found it. But I can truthfully report that for the most part she performed it very well and graciously. The house became deserted. I needn't go through all the programme ... I'll just tell you ... the most interesting and funny parts ...

... The playing of the General's Band. You'll remember that Mrs. Wilkinson taught them for a little while more than a year ago. Well, their instruments had gone out of tune again <u>badly</u> and they had forgotten their music, so that their rendering of the British and American anthems was enough to make a cat laugh and we stood only in deference to what was printed on the programme.

... The little blind girl's drill. They came from Nantai, wee tots, and did all sorts of pretty kindergarten games. At first they were shy and I thought their performance would collapse altogether, but they warmed up to it and forgot the audience and evoked rounds of applause.

> ... The Blind Boys Kindergarten drill which was very well done indeed and very pretty with colored handkerchiefs. The little fellows were all dressed in coats and long trousers to match, made of dark blue cloth covered with a white flower pattern.
>
> ... The flag drill by the bigger blind boys, each with 2 flags, one Chinese and one special blind school flag. They lined up at the end of their drill and sang the Chinese National Anthem.
>
> ... The English song and the band pieces by the Blind Boys Choir, which were splendid, as good as any Queen's Hall concert.
>
> The speech of the afternoon, your Mother's, was splendid, just exactly the right thing, but I can't attempt to give it to you word for word. It was translated into Chinese Mandarin ... the Foochow dialect being only for less illustrious uses.
>
> After the programme was over, came tea for <u>everybody</u>. They seemed to get heaps too without any fuss and as soon as they were finished they were all drafted over to the Blind Boys School to see over it and from there they departed ... I caught a glimpse of your mother before I went—simply beaming.[30]

Writing about the occasion later, Amy described the complimentary boards as six by two-and-a-half feet with beautifully composed characters. On one was written "Those who restore to others that which they lack are worthy of great honor." On a second, "Light, Clear, Brilliant, Help the world." And, on a third, written by the president of the republic in Chinese, on gold silk with an official seal: "It is an honor to the school to have received these marks of distinction from the Government, and their real value lies in the fact that they indicate the awakening of China to an appreciation of what is being done for the blind in Christ's name."[31]

News of Amy's awards hit Australian newspapers across the country, typical of which was one stating that "News has been received from Foochow, China, that the Chinese Government has just awarded the great honor of the Order of the Golden Grain to Mrs Wilkinson." It added that "prior to her leaving with Dr. Wilkinson for England on a well earned furlough, the military and civil governors of the Province presented Mrs Wilkinson with a special medal for good works."[32]

---

30. Welch, *Amy Oxley*, three-page item preceding Appendix 1.
31. Wilkinson, *Soul-Lighted School*, 5.
32. *Wagga Wagga Daily Advertiser*, 16 July 1920, 2.

6

From the Far East to the East End
(1921–1949)

AMY AND GEORGE COULD hardly wait to arrive in England to see their children. Even though they were returning a year earlier than expected, letters from Jane were weighing heavily upon them. Horace's death had abruptly cut off the steady income she and her mother relied on and they were not entitled to the military pension for spouses. The five-year arrangement for looking after the children was also coming to an end. Isabel had left school, and Marsden was about to enter secondary college. All this meant that some major decisions had to be made.

Through George's medical contacts, the Wilkinsons had organized to rent a house in Beaconsfield, on the rural edge of London. Despite selling their house in Kuliang, poor exchange rates had left them financially constrained. They soon realized that any further separation from their children was out of the question. Letters from them since Horace's death indicated that life under aunt Jane's rule had become increasingly strict. Isabel was missing her parents deeply, and Marsden was becoming something of a handful. For the sake of their children, Amy and George decided that returning to China was no longer an option. They needed to help Isabel find work as a nurse or governess and enroll Marsden in a school that would prepare him for university or a trade. Neither of these opportunities would be possible in Foochow. However much Amy and George's hearts still lay in China, they knew they had to resign.

In October, George wrote to CMS committees in both London and Fukien, citing "urgent family circumstances" as the reason for their decision.

Since there was no obvious replacement for George, they pleaded with him to return but he and Amy both felt it was God's timing to resign. At its next meeting in February, the Fukien Conference tabled the following resolution:

> It is with regret that we record the resignation of Dr. Wilkinson. During the twenty-one years that Dr. Wilkinson spent in this Mission he founded and developed the present CMS. Medical Mission. By his kindness and sympathy he won the love of many. As a surgeon he stood in the forefront of his profession and his services were sought for by man far and wide. We pray God that His blessing may ever be with our brother, and we feel sure that though he may no longer be with us, his keen interest in the work that he founded will continue, and we trust that he may be able to deepen and extend missionary interest at home.
>
> We wish to place on record our great appreciation of the work accomplished by Mrs Wilkinson for the Blind Boys School. She began her work and carried it to a very high standard of efficiency. Her name will always be connected with this splendid work. The Mission has sustained a very serious loss by her resignation and we sincerely hope she will be able to return to the field at a later date to continue this good work.[1]

There were other deep expressions of regret. In March, the editorial of the medical missionary journal *Mercy and Truth* recorded that: "Dr Wilkinson will long be remembered as a skillful surgeon by thousands of grateful Chinese patients, and Mrs Wilkinson has left an imperishable memorial to her loving labor in the Blind School."

In order to secure an income, George set up a private practice in the front rooms of their home at Beaconsfield. This occupied much of the following year and involved him entering into extended financial obligations. Amy found the adjustment to being mainly at home difficult, especially since in China there was always domestic help. She decided to put forward a proposal to CMS that the Foochow Blind School Band take part in the upcoming CMS "Africa and the East" Exhibition in London. This was accepted, and her setting up a schedule that included venues, accommodation, and publicity for the tour soon became a part-time job.

This first CMS Exhibition since the war, was to be held at the expansive Agricultural Hall in Islington from 17 May to 15 June, followed by brief tours to cities elsewhere in England. Its aim was to demonstrate "the worthwhileness of missionary work today" through displays of CMS work from various countries in Africa and Asia. In April, eight boys from the Blind

---

1. Minutes of Fukien Conference, February 192 in the Wilkinson Collection.

School, together with two assistants, set out from Foochow. An article in Singapore's *Straits Times* captures something of Amy's organizational skills in pulling off this ambitious vision.

> Eight boys from the School had arrived in England, having travelled by Japanese steamer via the Suez Canal—a longer journey than they had hitherto taken from their homeland. Each boy is a trained musician and can play and sing English and Chinese music. All can speak English to some level quite fluently. They were accompanied by their Chinese teacher . . . and by a coolie who cooks their food in native fashion.[2]

30 CMS Exhibition in the Agricultural Hall, London, 1922

This Exhibition was a huge event. Over five hundred ticket secretaries were required to process the crowds that attended—ultimately a quarter of a million people. The layout of the venue included partial replicas of an African village, a mission hospital, a Chinese street, an Indian outcast village, a Japanese rickshaw ride, and the Foochow Blind Boys Band.[3] As a headline entitled "Forty Truckloads of Scenery" recorded, the organization required to create the Chinese display, including the Blind School, was massive.

2. *Straits Times*, 6 June 1922, 10.
3. "Africa and the East," 1922.

> In the Chinese Street we see members of the blind boys band from the 'Soul-Lighted School' at Foochow, all happily at work making mats and baskets. Then we listen to one of their concerts in the Chinese Guest Room . . . We can only mention the very interesting cinema lectures, costumes, scenes and other attractions of this fine exhibition.[4]

From the start of the Exhibition, reports of the 'Chinese Street' display began to capture people's imagination. As the bishop of London commented:

> I came in for a quarter of an hour; I have now spent 3 hours here and I see already that I must revise all my ideas of foreign missions. Early publicity of the varied activities in the China Street display helped draw crowds to it:
>
> > For these lads are a little bit of the real China . . . As you look at them you have to realise that they are representative and symbolic of many thousands of the blind in China for whom in the past practically no provision has been made. They are living testimonies of what the coming of the Lord Jesus Christ means to the 'sick', to the 'lost' of these vast populations of the East; once unwanted and neglected they have been cared for, educated, saved in the wide and true sense of the word.
> >
> > The performance, consisting of vocal and instrumental music in English and Chinese we attended was received with the utmost appreciation by a large audience . . . Mrs Wilkinson is anxious that English audiences should understand and feel the force of the Gospel message which these young men are singing, and certainly their songs do linger in the mind.
> >
> > Mrs Wilkinson herself, through her Christly work as foundress of the Boys' Blind School, and as guardian mother to these dear lads now in our country is an effective argument for the Christian Mission.[5]

---

4. *Children's Newspaper*, 3 June 1922, 2, reported in 'Look and Learn Magazine,' www.lookandlearn.com.

5. Guage, "Remarkable Missionary Exhibition," *United Methodist*, May 1922, 248.

From the Far East to the East End (1921–1949)

31 Amy being presented to Queen Mary at the CMS Exhibition, 1922

For Amy, the highlight of the month-long event was being presented to Her Majesty, Queen Mary, during an official visit to the Exhibition on 30 May. The monarch was fascinated by the Chinese displays, asked questions about the work of the school and its band, and complimented Amy on her role in developing these. Of particular interest to her was the blind boys' skills in music and trades, especially matting. The queen graciously accepted one of the mats presented to her by Amy on behalf of the school.[6]

While the Exhibition was taking place, the CMS committee in Fukien wrote to George urging his return as soon as possible. His successor, Dr. Ding, had unexpectedly died, and they had been unable find anyone to replace him. George replied that, partly because he had entered into a financial contract connected with his practice, he could not do this. The committee then pressured the CMS Medical Mission in London to help resolve this problem. Though it offered to cover George's financial liabilities by providing £100 annually for the next five years, his reply to Fukien was unequivocal.

6 Reported in the *Daily Express*, 31 July 1922, as well as the *Church Missionary Outlook*, July 1922, 149.

> It is very hard, on behalf of my wife and myself, to have again to say 'No' . . . We greatly appreciate the effort . . . to make matters smooth for us financially. The question is however much more than a financial one and involves problems which seem to us unsolvable. With appreciation of the great need at Foochow and deep sympathy with our fellow-workers there, we can see no gleam pointing us Chinawards.[7]

For Amy, the Exhibition was only the starting point of a five-month, five thousand mile tour of one hundred and thirty cities and towns across England. Events were generally held in large public venues such as town or guild halls (including the famous Grand Pump Room in Bath), in parks, gardens, on piers, and occasionally in large churches or chapels. There were often afternoon and evening concerts, with separate performances for children and adults. Performances were publicized beforehand in regional newspapers, and reported on afterwards in considerable detail.

Travel was mainly by charabanc, a large open-air vehicle holding up to twelve passengers. Accommodation was mainly provided by well-off local CMS members, including one stay in a bishop's residence. The tour began from Carlisle in the north, down through the Midlands, Wales, and Devon, to Kent and the South Coast. Some of the cities visited were Sunderland, York, Derby, Gloucester, Chelmsford, Bath, Bristol, Exeter, Barnstaple, Hastings, and Dover.

The fullest account of a typical performance comes from the *Dover Express* under the banner "Blind Chinese Boys Concert."[8]

> There was a very large attendance at the Town Hall on Monday evening to listen to the programme provided by the blind Chinese boy musicians from Foochow, where a school has been run for 25 years by Mrs G. Wilkinson, who brought the party to England in order that more may be known of this highly successful missionary work.
>
> The Mayor . . . said that it was a great pleasure to him to be able to welcome to Dover the blind lads from China, and he was sure the audience would join with him in that especially when they remembered the instruments the lads played they had never seen nor the music . . . they were all taught to read and were able to go out into the world to earn their own living. Already some were married and had children . . . It was seldom [people] had the chance to see the result of money sent abroad, and, therefore, they were especially gratified to be able

---

7. Both documents are in the Wilkinson Collection.
8. *Dover Express,* 21 July 1922, 14.

to be present that evening. He gave the boys a hearty welcome to Dover (applause).

Mrs Wilkinson said she thanked them very much for the reception given to the boys. She could assure them that it was a great privilege and honor to come to the old town of Dover.

The programme which followed was exceptionally well carried out, and the explanation by Mrs Wilkinson as to the various methods of teaching, added greatly to the interest. The playing of the Chinese cymbals at the outset made the audience wonder what was to follow, but any fear they might have had was soon dispelled, however, by 'The Double Eagle', a march played by the band in fine style. The rendering of the 23rd Psalm, first in Chinese and then in English, was an item equally well received, the enunciation of the reader in English being very good and gave some idea of the excellent training they received in the school. These items were followed by others equally good, a hymn in Chinese, 'Lord, I care not for riches', and on the stringed instruments 'Unkind friends receive a bad reward.' On the organ one of the party played with considerable feeling 'What are these arrayed with white?' and he was loudly applauded at the close. 'Killarney' was a well-rendered cornet solo; and a quartette in English 'Is it well with thy soul?' was much appreciated.

32 The Blind Boys Band that toured England, 1922

The Mayor, appealing for generous contributions to the collection, said that there was one point which had appealed to him that evening from Mrs Wilkinson's remarks, and that was the opportunity they had of trade with China . . . [and] would not only receive benefit themselves but China would also do so.

During the taking of the collection, the band played the march 'Men of Harlech' and afterwards Mrs Wilkinson described the trades which the boys were learning and some of their training in school, showing some of the mats which they had made, one of which had been accepted by Her Majesty the Queen.

The Rev E.E. Brown thanked the Mayor and Mayoress for being present and also the party which had provided such a splendid entertainment. He was certain the hearers had been touched by what they had seen and heard. He asked that they should give the lads a hearty clap.

At the request of a member of the audience the hymn 'When peace like a river' was sung at the close.[9]

Other newspaper accounts indicate the presence of local aristocracy and professional people at these events. Typical comments about the evening include reference to the "beautiful singing," "novel instruments," "extraordinary entertainment," and "impressive reading of Scripture." There is frequent mention of "very large attendance," "every seat being occupied," "general applause," and an "enthusiastic response." Particular items, for example a boy singing "And I shall see my Pilot's face when I have crossed the bar," were reported to have evoked deep "pathos and sympathy" in those listening. Concertgoers waited afterwards to see the band, "cheering them as they left for their quarters," and observed that the boys were "soul-lighted, though they cannot see, living witnesses to the power of Christianity."

A farewell concert was held on 29 January 1923 at the Queen's Hall in London. Many CMS supporters and Exhibition stewards attended. To these people, "there came once more, against the background of China's overwhelming need and magnificent possibilities, a vision of the whole world's need . . . and the life of service open to every Christian."[10]

Although for Amy it was exhausting, the blind boys' tour had been a wonderful opportunity. Many across England gained firsthand experience of the importance of mission. The boys increased their confidence in performing in English, developed additional skills in piano tuning, and learned

---

9. Spontaneous contributions from audiences were not uncommon at this time, even in large gatherings.

10. *Church Missionary Outlook*, 1 March 1923, 60.

the new trades of shoemaking and massage to take back and teach at the school. Ticket sales from their performances would contribute substantially to the school's financial security over the coming years. As she said farewell to the band in early February, Amy wondered if she would ever see her "Chinese boys" again? A number had been her first students and others she had personally taught. All hearts were heavy as they prayed together on the docks for the final time.

On the band's return trip, while waiting in Hong Kong for a connecting boat to Foochow, the band played again in Kowloon. An Australian missionary in Foochow, Nellie Matthews, provided the following snapshot of what the English tour meant to the Blind School.

> There was great excitement and real joy among all in the Blind School when the boys arrived from England. They were so well and happy . . . Now each mail brings them letters from their English friends, sometimes written in English Braille. Of course the blind boys can answer all letters themselves by typewriter or in Braille . . . The boys feel they cannot say enough about the kindness of the English people, and they say, 'Truly it was not because of our music, it was not because we play and sing well that the people were so kind to us: no, truly our music and singing is nothing compared with the music they have in England; it is because they have received the real Christian teaching and reckon us fellow Christians, as brothers, that they loved us and treated us kindly.[11]

This was a bright counterpoint to wider social and political developments that had been taking place in China. Protests against the West that had first surfaced before Amy and George's departure had been strengthened by university student unrest and the emergence of the Communist Party. And although the Communists had joined the Nationalist Kuomintang Party under Sun Yat Sen, the relationship was an uneasy one. Worsening economic conditions and food shortages lead to further disturbances, including Foochow in 1924. At times like these, the Blind School was reliant on food packages distributed through CMS from England. It also received donations from churches and schools in Australia.[12] From 1926, a series

11. Op. cit., p. 56.
12. See further the reports in *The Sun,* 31 October 1924, 14, and *The Register,* 15

of larger demonstrations, which sometimes turned violent, took place in Foochow. Some of these arose among students in educational institutions like Trinity College: others were caused by soldiers coming from outside the province. During these disturbances, several Christian organisations in the Old City, including the Blind School, were attacked.

> On the day of the looting the soldiers went to the Blind School three times, and this is how they were parried. The boys bravely stood around the gate and each time the soldiers came the head boy, who has one sighted eye, was there ready. He assured them that there were no foreigners on the premises. "You see," he said, "we are all blind, and very poor, I am the manager of this place, and these blind people make matting here—there are no foreigners here at all. If you want to come in, please choose a few of your number—you could not all come—I will show a small party of you the whole place." . . They looked into every corner, and seeing no signs of foreigners or foreigner's things, they left, but they told the head boy they would kill him if they did find that any foreigners were there.[13]

Early the next year, more violent protests took place. The Blind School was looted, the buildings wrecked, and pupils turned out into the streets. The temporary head of the school, and his wife were on site, but fortunately they managed to escape. In early May, soldiers were again involved in looting and robbing a number of Christian institutions, including the nurses' and doctors' quarters at Cha Cang Hospital. These disturbances led to missionaries being evacuated from the City for the remainder of the year. The military commander in Foochow first arrested, and then executed, two hundred agitators involved in outrages against missionaries.[14] During that time, the hospital was run by the Chinese staff alone. Both institutions recovered when life settled down in early 1928. The hospital opened new buildings, and the school moved to the Western-style Medical University. By then Rev Norton had returned as principal and all eight of the students who had toured England were teachers at the school.[15]

September 1924, 12.

13. *Daily Express* (Griffith, NSW), 21 May 1927, 2.

14. *The Sun*, 29 January 1927, 1.

15. On these two incidents, see respectively *Straits Times*, 4 February 1927, 10 (Singapore) and *Evening News*, 11 May 1927, 9 (Sydney). On the general growth and progress of the hospital around this time, see the report by Baldwin, *The Mission Hospital*, November 1928, 292–94.

> In 1925 Sun Yat Sen died, and General Chiang Kai Shek was appointed leader of the Kuomintang. Because of the latter's influence, two years later the smaller Communist faction broke away and based themselves in the countryside rather than cities. Starting from Canton, Chiang's forces began a major military expedition to defeat the ruling conservative Nationalists in the north. On the way they passed through Foochow and, after some heavy fighting, were ultimately victorious. They established a new capital in Nanking and installed Chaing as the country's new leader. He initiated laws requiring the transfer of power in schools and hospitals into Chinese hands. With his Western-educated wife's help, he gained support from several Western countries and sped up the modernization of China.

In the spring of 1930, terrifying news reached Amy and George about two of their friends, CMS missionaries Eleanor Harrison and Edith Nettleton, who worked at a school in the mountainous north of the province. The two women had been kidnapped by bandits who had loose links with the Communists. English and Australian newspapers were filled with confusing accounts of their plight. As they were making a trip down the Min River to the capital, they had been captured and a ransom of half a million dollars demanded. Through the British consul, CMS offered to pay part of this sum for their release.

While negotiations were taking place, these sixty-year-old women were subjected to physical and mental brutalities. They were guarded around the clock by four captors and constantly harassed by depictions of the terrible fate that awaited them. When their captors received word of the reduced payment, one of Eleanor's fingers was cut off and forwarded to Foochow. Then, without waiting for a response, on 1 September she and four Chinese prisoners were given a lengthy, farcical trial. At its conclusion, one of the Chinese was shot and the remaining three beheaded. While her captors waited for a response to their renewed demands, Eleanor's sentence was reprieved, but Edith was told that she would suffer the same fate if the full amount was not paid. A few later, before a response could arrive, the two were taken to an isolated house on a hillside and beheaded. A letter written by their captors stated: "We have power to take you foreigners, hold you to ransom, and kill you."[16] For Amy, memories flooded back as she read about how her friends' bodies were eventually found and taken to Foochow for burial beside the other martyrs at Kucheng.

---

16. *Albury Banner*, 19 December 1930, 34.

In planning the tour of the Blind Boys Band, Amy had established many contacts within the British Embassy in London. Once these officials realized her language skills, she was regularly asked to help Chinese seeking assistance in understanding and filling out documents, looking for employment, and making use of community services.

> As a result of the East India Company's trade in tea, silks, and ceramics from China, the number of Chinese living in London grew significantly. A typical permanent resident, mostly from southern China, would sign on as a crew member in Hong Kong and then jump ship in London with the intention of working hard to send money back to their extended family. By the late nineteenth century, they had settled across the dockland areas of Limehouse and Pennyfields, living on streets with names like Amoy Place and Ming Street. Many opened up shops, restaurants, and laundries. Alongside these reputable businesses were not-so-reputable ones catering to sailors' favorite pastimes—prostitution, gambling, and smoking opium. Since most of their wives remained in China, many of them moved in with British women. As these knew they would lose their citizenship if they married a foreigner, most mixed couples simply cohabited. The city was also the base for a sizeable floating population of sailors who were between ships,[17] as well as a growing number of Chinese students who had travelled to London for study.

---

17. "The Chinese in Britain (United Kingdom) History Timeline," Zakkeith.com, viewed August 2015.

33 Chinese in Limehouse during the 1930s

Amy felt sure that God was opening up a new way of serving the Chinese people. Her embassy contacts had connected her with the Chinese community in the East End: "since 1923 a good deal of my time has been spent in work for the Chinese, both in the Embassy and among students—also a definite work for Chinese seamen, their wives and families and those who have married English wives, and their children."[18] As well as visiting these people in their homes, for the next six years Amy hired a local hall in Pennyfields and set up English language classes, children's clubs, Scouts and Cubs, Sunday School, and church services. For this work she seems to have been paid a small stipend by both the British Embassy and the London Chinese Evangelical Mission. Part of the genius of her approach was training a team of voluntary helpers. By the early 1930s she was reaching up to three thousand men, women, and children a year. The growth of the work encouraged the Mission to hire two larger rooms in Gower Street where

---

18. Wilkinson, for The Berrima Historical Society, unnumbered.

Amy often preached on Sundays. Through these services and her personal contacts, many people came forward for baptism.[19]

On the home front, in 1930 Isabel went to India as a nanny employed by a British army expat family, and Marsden began work as a trainee manager. Amy and George decided to move to Ealing, as this was closer to George's new group practice in Fulham. In the following years, their home became a haven of hospitality to many Chinese people.

> There were those... who would come and see me, Chinese cadets would come up from their ships for a day and a night, and (once) a Chinese radar officer spent three weeks in our house. One steward on board keeps me informed of the dates of his ports of call, from the Persian Gulf, Hong Kong, Singapore, Shanghai, Western Australia, Tasmania and lastly of Sydney—I send him books and he sends me letters and sometimes rice, to share when my Chinese friends visit me.[20]

A succession of CIM workers, either setting out for, or on furlough from, China also lived in their house for longer periods. These included a mix of serving and new missionaries, including William Drew, whom Amy mentored while he assisted her at the Gower Street Mission.

Alongside his medical practice, on weekends George helped in the Mission. Since opium addiction was an issue in Chinatown, his experience in Fukien was occasionally called on. Around this time, the Gilead Medical Mission, which had a link with CMS, asked if he would work voluntarily in a dispensary for Jewish people in Fournier Street, Spitalfields. In the 1930s, this area was predominantly made up of poorer, Jewish, working-class people. The Mission encountered strong opposition from Jewish community leaders, particularly for its work among women and children, some of whom showed interest in midweek meetings held in the same building. However, the dire needs of the East End during the Depression were so severe that these leaders largely turned a blind eye to what was happening. The Mission stood out among the predominantly garment-making businesses with the words "Jeshua said I am the way, the truth and the life" painted on its facade.

Meanwhile in India, taking advantage of her new-found freedom, Isabel quickly adjusted to expat living, enjoying the travel and social life in Bombay. Not long after her arrival she met Geoffrey Hazelton,

---

19. Wilkinson, for The Berrima Historical Society, unnumbered.
20. Wilkinson, for The Berrima Historical Society, unnumbered.

a very young officer in the British Army who had been invited to a tea party at the house of one of his commanding officers and had been instructed to dress for tennis. He arrived feeling very hot and nervous late in the afternoon. As he was shown out to the court he saw a young lady playing a match. Captivated he said 'There she was, this tiny little thing with flaming red hair, laughing and laughing.' It was not long before he proposed and had to change his regiment because his own would not give young officers permission to marry.[21]

Their wedding took place in London in November 1932. A year later Marsden married Elizabeth (Betty) Trace. With the birth of Isabel and Geoffrey's first child, Peter, the same year, Amy and George became grandparents. It was several years before Marsden and Betty had a child, whom they named Shuna. Amy enjoyed being a grandmother and doing fun things with the children.

During the 1930s, Amy and George continually received news about developments in China. They were relieved to hear that life was now more settled in Foochow as a result of Chiang Kai Shek's leadership. A radio station had opened in Foochow, and within a few years every second house in the city had its own wireless. One was donated to the Blind School.[22] It was occasionally invited to come into the radio station to record a musical program containing religious content. Every Christmas, a special carol service and sermon was broadcast across the whole of Fukien Province.

Despite the earlier disruptions, Cha Cang—now renamed Christ's—Hospital continued to expand. There were now several doctors, additional nurses, and two new midwives. In London in 1933, the annual meeting of the Medical Mission Auxiliary of CMS rated the training of nurses in China as the best among its fifty-four hospitals throughout the world. The advanced medical treatment of tuberculosis in four of the hospitals, including Christ's, was also highly praised.[23] As the pioneer of these kinds of

---

21. This reminiscence was provided in a personal letter from Ruth Oxley Horne, Isabel's granddaughter.
22. *Church Missionary Outlook*, December 1934, 8, and *Eastward Ho*, December 1933, 186. A few years later the School also received copies of the new hymn book for use in churches, as the second of these two magazines reported in its July 1937, 108.
23. *Singapore Press and Mercantile Advertiser*, 29 May 1933, 12.

developments, George felt especially gratified.[24] A couple of years later, he and Amy read that two friends, the current Anglican bishop and the ex-principal of the Blind School, were both optimistic about the new life emerging in Fukien Province. Though Christians had experienced much suffering over the decades—from the Hwasang massacre to the present—more of the Chinese elite, and more people in unreached parts of the province, were being reached by the gospel.[25]

34 Amy, wearing her Order of the Golden Grain and Viceroy's Medals, c. 1930

Amy and George continued to be visited by people they knew in Fukien. Every few years they caught up with a CMS missionary on furlough from the province, someone connected to the work of the school or hospital, or a particular colleague with whom they had a close connection. One of these was our relative Sophie Newton who, with fellow CMS missionary Marion Onyon, visited Amy in October 1937. The following letter provides one of the few, if brief, firsthand descriptions of Amy's work among the Chinese in London.

24. Suggestions were also being made about the need to standardize and professionalize teaching of the blind in China. See Wong, *And There Was Light*, 58ff.

25. See issues of the *Church Missionary Outlook* for October 1935, 1–2, and March 1937, 49–51, respectively.

We alighted at 7.30pm. Mrs Wilkinson met us and we did so enjoy those who help her. A nice earnest young man is Cub Master and is doing a splendid work among the boys, and this was the third anniversary. The cubs are nearly all half-castes and children of sailors. Later on, the Scouts met. We met the Chinese Evangelist, Mr Chen, who comes from Ningpo and his English wife who works among women and children. It was good to be in Chinatown and see the characters all over the walls. But I must tell you it took well over an hour to get home and yet Mrs Wilkinson has regularly to take one and a half hours by tube and bus to reach the house—she is the same zealous, enthusiastic, worker she ever was, and loves those boys. On Sunday we had a delightful afternoon at the house and met three Chinese students (one English history, one journalism, one philosophy—clever and so nice to talk to). Also a Chinese born in Jamaica (who can't speak Chinese), a nurse four years in Liverpool and now in a London Hospital, such a dear—a Mrs Lim (a doctor's wife) from Singapore so young and charming—and both so perfectly natural ... We had tea ... then we set to work to start rolling bandages in order to help China and also in response to Madam Chiang Kai Shek's plea for help. It was beautiful to see how ready the young men were to roll bandages ... then we went round together to a Baptist Church nearby where Mrs Wilkinson knows the gospel is faithfully preached, as the students are not all Christians.[26]

In her letter, Sophie also mentioned the concern expressed by the Chinese at the recent Japanese offensive against Fukien.

> In July 1937, the Japanese army began an undeclared war on China near Peking. A month later, the Chinese government ordered the evacuation of Japanese residents from several cities, including Foochow. The Nationalist and Communist forces combined in a popular front to resist the invaders. Several northern cities, including Peking, Shanghai, and the capital Nanking, fell to the Japanese. Tens of thousands of innocent civilians were killed in the wake of their victories, such as the horrific slaughter known as "the Rape of Nanking."

In May 1938, the city of Amoy fell to the Japanese, threatening the security of nearby Foochow. Then, at the beginning of June, three Chinese gunboats in the estuary of the Min were bombed and sunk. The naval barracks, shipyard, and hospital near the Pagoda Anchorage were blown up,

---

26. Letter dated 29 September 1937 in the Banks Family Collection.

and that section of the city fell to Japanese forces.²⁷ Amy and George were understandably anxious about their ex-colleagues in the capital, as well as the boys and patients in the school and hospital.

However, they soon had more immediate concerns. After the "calm before the storm" in the opening months of the war, the fall of the first bombs on central London changed life as they knew it. As well as seeking to erode morale before a German invasion, the Blitz was designed to paralyze commercial life by targeting docks and nearby warehouses, railway lines, factories, and power stations. During September 1940 and May 1941, 25,000 tons of bombs left much of the East End in ruins and drove most Chinese residents to relocate a few miles away in Soho. This marked the beginning of the final chapter of Amy's work with the Chinese.

Amid these events, Amy and George became grandparents again with the birth of Isabel's second son, David. As this took place in South Africa, where Isabel was safely located with other officers' wives while their husbands were away fighting in Palestine, Amy didn't see her new grandson until he was three. However Peter, who was eleven at this time, recounts various stories about his grandma. On one occasion, he went with her to a Chinese restaurant in Soho and all the staff and diners stood up to show their respect as she entered the room. On another occasion, when bombs fell near their house in Putney during the war, Amy prayed on her knees while he tried to peek through the blackout curtains!²⁸ At the same time in Foochow, Japanese planes were dropping bombs near the Blind School and Christ's Hospital, fortunately without loss of life. Later in that conflict, however, both the school and hospital were ransacked and badly damaged.²⁹ Only with the Japanese surrender in May 1945 did peace finally return to Foochow.

In the closing years of the war, several pressures weighed heavily upon Amy. Now in her late seventies, she was feeling the strain of both the war and death of almost all her siblings as well as many of her friends. George's health also started to decline, and by 1946 he was showing the signs of Alzheimer's disease. It became impossible for Amy to leave the house for any length of time. To help his parents out, Marsden and his family moved into a three-storied residence in central Ealing with his parents and shared the rent. How well this arrangement worked out, we don't know. In any case, at the end of 1948, Marsden was offered a management position in Sydney by

---

27. On this period refer Hackett, "Imperial Japanese Navy and China."

28. These stories were passed on by his daughter Ruth Horne.

29. A report by Bishop Michael Chang was contained in *The Church Missionary Outlook*, October 1945, 3.

the jewelery company he was working for in London. As this position had long-term prospects, he decided to emigrate with his family as part of the assisted program offered by the Australian government.

By the beginning of 1949, Amy, now 81, was feeling tired. With Isabel and Geoffrey still away—this time in Hong Kong, where Geoffrey took up a high-ranking military post after receiving an Order of the British Empire award—she was also feeling isolated. By March that year, Amy learned that she had cancer of the liver. As this was already advanced, immediate palliative care was necessary. The only available option was Bethany Nursing Home, some distance away in Tunbridge Wells. During her final few weeks, one of the things that occupied her mind and prayers was the fate of her school in China. If victorious, the Communists had threatened to eradicate Christianity and expel missionaries from the country. This could lead to persecution of the boys, especially those who had spent time in the West, and ultimately to the closure of the school.

Amy died on 6 June. Her funeral was conducted in the chapel at Tunbridge Wells cemetery, and she was buried nearby. The *Fukien News* carried the following "In Memoriam":

> Since our last issue there has passed from us to higher service [an] outstanding personality of the church in Fukien. Amy Wilkinson's name is known to a very wide circle of friends and supporters through the wonderful work she did for blind boys and men. The School for Blind Boys that grew out of her inspired sympathy from its beginnings in Lieng Kong to a fine institution of many and varied activities in Foochow City is a splendid memorial to her life. But better still is the love and veneration in the hearts of many boys and men saved by her from lives of misery to lives of useful and joyful service. Surely in her ears must have sounded the Master's words 'Inasmuch as you did it to the least of these my brethren, you did it to Me.'[30]

After Amy's funeral, Isabel organized for George to live in Winscombe Retirement Home in Gerards Cross. As this was set up to cater for doctors, she knew he would be well looked after. Geoffrey had decided to leave the army to train for the Anglican ministry, and the Home was not too far from the theological college where he would be studying.[31] During this time, George often reflected on the legacy of his work in China. He took heart

---

30. *Fukien News*, 4 November 1949, 4–5. The Bible quotation is from Matthew 25:40.

31. This move was a result of the influence of Anglican bishop Ronald Hall of Hong Kong.

from an address by the CMS General Secretary entitled "Looking Back and Going Forward." There was no need to be discouraged, he wrote, especially about what was happening in Fukien, as it would give Christians there the opportunity to show that their faith was genuinely Chinese and not a Western import. "Can you see," he asked, "that all this fits into what you read about China in the papers? That it may even be part of God's plan?"[32]

This echoed the words of Bishop Michael Chang in 1950, on the centenary of Christian work in Foochow.

> We are afraid that your hearts may be heavy, as you think of the end, as it may seem, of all the endeavor to which you gave so much; and we should like to say a few words about that . . . if circumstances outside our control should bring to an end after 100 years the work of missionaries among us, it is not the end; for not only does what you have built abide, but so also does the determination to remain in fellowship with you, and to make that fellowship real to us all in whatever ways may be possible.[33]

These words gave George comfort as he thought about the future. On 18 November 1951, aged eighty-six, he died, and was buried next to his beloved wife and co-worker of forty-seven years. The inscription on two Bible-shaped headstones, resting side by side, captures forever where their hearts truly belonged.

> Amy Wilkinson
> Founder
> CMS Blind Boys School
> Died 6 June 1949
> Aged 81
>
> George Wilkinson
> Founder
> Foochow Mission Hospital
> Died 18 November 1951
> Aged 86

---

32. See the *Church Missionary Outlook*, July 1950, 8, and the *Fukien News*, November 1949, 10.

33. *Church Missionary Outlook*, December 1950, 4–5.

Afterword

In October 2016, we landed in Hong Kong airport to meet up with our travelling companions for ten days in Fuzhou. Ruth Horne, Amy and George's great granddaughter, and her husband Brian met us in the departure lounge for the hour long flight. All four of us were nervous and excited at what lay ahead. On arrival we discovered that our hotel rooms looked out across the Min River to Nantai Island.

The next morning we were driven to the new campus of the, now co-educational, Fuzhou Blind School to be distinguished guests at their Annual International White Cane Day celebration. At the gates was a small honor guard of girls in colourful uniforms. We were then greeted warmly by the principal, staff and board members as well as by our translator, Dr. Jihong. Together they showed us some of the expansive buildings and grounds on the campus.

When we entered the main auditorium, the audience of several hundred people rose to their feet and applauded. As we looked around, we noticed students, teachers, parents, alumnae and others from the wider community. All were especially excited to have Amy's great granddaughter as the guest of honor. To our delight, the program began with a band, consisting of both girls and boys this time, followed by an ex-student singing, in Chinese, "Auld Lang Syne." As the concert went on, we were treated to items from infants to graduates who were now national celebrities, one of whom had won the Chinese equivalent of the "X Factor"! The blind students often spontaneously interacted with the performers in all kinds of ways—clapping, swaying, beating time, tapping their feet, and singing enthusiastically.

By far the loudest applause was for an item by five members of the school who were part of China's national blind football team. They had recently returned from the Rio Paralympics where their team just missed out on a bronze medal. Before the concert, we had been treated to an exhibition of some of their amazing skills on the school's oval, where Ruth and Brian played blindfold football with them. All the students seemed incredibly "at home" and happy, and there was an obviously close bond between them and their teachers, some of whom were blind themselves. We felt that Amy would have loved to have been there and we sensed her spirit hovering over the whole event. Throughout our visit, her name was often respectfully mentioned and her picture displayed on notice boards in the main reception area.

At the end of the concert, we joined key past and present staff, several older students and some distinguished alumnae over morning tea. There we exchanged stories and photos from our research. The oldest surviving alumnus shared memories of his own teacher, the cornet player in the Blind Boys Band that had toured England. The most delightful surprise was being shown the impressive medallion presented to Amy after the Nanking Exhibition in 1910.

We also found out more about the history of the school after the communist victory. In July 1951, the Boys and Girls Schools were merged and the premises moved to Cangshan on Nantai Island. With the expulsion of missionaries, its administration was transferred to a local government organisation. Over the next two decades, it underwent changes in name, leadership, and policy. Nevertheless, the school continued to make products and participate in sports, winning medals in provincial, national, and occasionally international competitions. During this period, little is known of any ongoing Australian connection with the school, but in 1986 Mary Andrews, the former principal of Deaconess House in Sydney, a former CMS missionary in China, visited and recorded its choir. In the 1990s, the current president of the People's Republic of China, Xi Jinping, then secretary of Fuzhou's Municipal Party Committee, personally supported the building of a new campus for the Blind School because of his deep interest in education.[1]

Despite no longer being a Christian institution, the imagery of light continues to be a vital part of the school's mission statement. As one stanza of the school's song echoes:

> 'Church Mission School', 'The Light Path' is my pride,
> Fuzhou Blind School makes us feel proud;
> With a more spiritual outlook,
> A better life will be created.

Over the next few days, we visited the key places where Amy and George lived and worked, some of them fast decaying and others now redeveloped. A highlight was a day spent at Kuliang in the mountains above the

---

1. See further *Fu Zhou Shi Mang Xiao*, especially 10–11.

city, where for the first time we discovered the location of the Wilkinson's summer house. We showed Ruth and Brian the hospital near North Gate, now the second largest in the city, and the surrounding area that once housed the early Blind School; the places in Kuliang where the Wilkinsons lived, relaxed, and socialized; the foreign concessions area on Nantai Island where they were married and spent time with missionary colleagues; the site of the church they attended where Ruth's grandmother was baptized; and the nearby oldest church in the city, which now has ten thousand members a week, where we gave a talk on Amy's life to their English language class.

Amy and George's graves in Tunbridge Wells

As our time in Fuzhou came to an end, we reflected on our recent visit to Amy and George's graves in Tunbridge Wells. On that beautiful sunny afternoon, in a quiet corner of the cemetery, we read aloud these words from the Bible that expressed the vision that shaped their life and work together.

> I saw a "new heaven and a new earth" . . . and the Holy City, the new Jerusalem coming down out of heaven from God, prepared as a bride beautifully dressed for her husband. And I heard a loud voice from the throne saying, "Look, God's dwelling place is now among the people, and he will dwell with them. They will be his people, and God himself will be with them and be their God. He will wipe every tear from their eyes. There will be no more death or mourning or crying or pain, for the old order of things has passed away."

He who was seated on the throne said, "I am making everything new!" ...

Then the angel showed me the river of the water of life, as clear as crystal, flowing from the throne of God down the middle of the great street of the city. On each side of the river stood the tree of life . . . And the leaves of the tree are for the healing of the nations. No longer will there be any curse. The throne of God and of the Lamb will be in the city, and his servants will serve him. They will see his face and his name will be on their foreheads. There will be no more night . . . for the Lord God will give them light. And they will reign for ever and ever.[2]

---

2. Revelation 21:1–5; 22:1–5.

Bibliography

"An Overview of the Chinese Expositions during the Late Qing Dynasty—An Article Celebrating China's First Ever World Expo." *Wikipedia*. http://en.wikipedia.org.

A Souvenir of "Africa and the East" CMS Exhibition, Agricultural Hall, 17 May to 15 June, 1922.

Banks, Linda, and Robert Banks. *Through the Valley of the Shadow: Australian Women in War-torn China*. Studies in Chinese Christianity. Eugene, OR: Pickwick Publications, 2019.

Banks, Robert. "The Influence of the Keswick Movement on the Transmission of Christianity in China." *Lucas* Series 2/9 (2015–16) 49–72.

Banks, Robert, and Linda Banks. *View from the Faraway Pagoda: A Pioneer Australian Missionary in China from the Boxer Rebellion to the Communist Insurgency*. Melbourne: Acorn, 2013.

Bays, Daniel H. *A New History of Christianity in China*. Blackwell Guides to Global Christianity. Malden, MA: Wiley-Blackwell, 2012.

Beard, W. L. Collection in Yale University Library. libraryyale.edu/divinitycontent/beard/Beard1913.

"Blindness Is a Public Health Issue in China." http://www.who.int/mediacentre/factsheets/fs230/en/.

Chant, Barry. *The Spirit of Pentecost: The Origin and Development of the Pentecostal Movement in Australia 1870–1930*. Adelaide: Emeth, 2011.

Church Missionary Society Archives. *Annual Letters of Missionaries, Church Missionary Gleaner, Church Missionary Intelligencer, Church Missionary Outlook, CMS Home Gazette, Eastward Ho, Extracts from Annual Reports, Mercy and Truth*. In Adam Matthews Digital Publications. https://www.amdigital.co.uk/primary-sources/church-missionary-society-archive/.

Codrington, Florence I. *Bring-Brother: One of the Children-in-Blue from the Town of Lone Bamboo*. London: Church of England Zenana Missionary Society, 1919.

Cole, E. Keith. *A History of the Church Missionary Society of Australia*. Melbourne: Church Missionary Society Historical Publications, 1971.

Dickey, Brian. ed. *The Australian Dictionary of Evangelical Biography*. Sydney: Evangelical Historical Association, 1994.

Dictionary of Sydney, 2008. http://www.dictionaryofsydney.org/entry/Kirkham.

Dunch, Ryan. *Fuzhou Protestants and the Making of a Modern China 1857–1927*. New Haven: Yale University Press, 2001.

Dunlop, E. W. "Oxley, John Joseph (1784-1828)." In *The Australian Dictionary of Biography* (ADB). National Centre of Biography, Australian National University: http://adb.anu.edu.au/biography/oxley-johnjoseph,2530/text3431/.
"Eliza Hassall." *Illawarra Historical Society* (2 March/April, 1999).
Fagg, May. *Two Golden Lilies from the Empire of the Rising Sun.* 1920?. Reprint, London: Forgotten Books, 2011.
Fu Zhou Shi Mang Xiao. Fuzhou: Fuzhou Blind School, 2010.
Goodman, Ruth. *How to Be a Victorian.* London: Penguin, 2013.
Grubb, Norman. *C.T. Studd: Cricketer and Pioneer.* London: Lutterworth, 1933.
Hackett, Bob. "Rising Storm: The Imperial Japanese Navy and China." www.combined%eet.com/Fuzhou_t/htm/.
Harford, C. F. "The Climate of the CMS Mission Fields: XI Foochow." *Mercy and Truth* (November 1909) 56–59.
Hassall, James. S. *In Old Australia: Records and Reminiscences from 1794.* 1902. Reprint, North Sydney: Library of Australian History, 1977.
Hsu, I. C. Y. *The Rise of Modern China.* 5th ed. New York: Oxford University Press, 1995.
Hope, Alistair and Ellen. Family Collection. For Diary and Letters of Isabel Hope.
Ibbotson, Mary E. et al. *Everyday Tales of China.* London: Church Missionary Society, 1950?
Johnson, Richard. *The Search for the Inland Sea: John Oxley, Explorer.* Melbourne: Melbourne University Press, 2001.
Johnston, James. *China and Formosa: The Story of the Mission of the Presbyterian Church of England.* London: Hazell, Watson & Viney, 1897.
Johnstone, Samuel M. *Samuel Marsden: A Pioneer of Civilization in the South Seas.* Sydney: Angus & Robertson, 1932.
Keen, Gordon. *A Short History of China: From Ancient Dynasties to Economic Powerhouse.* Harpenden: Pocket Essentials, 2013.
Lee, Joseph T.-H. *The Bible and the Gun: Christianity in South China 1860–1900.* New York: Routledge, 2001.
Lovell, Julia. *The Opium War: Drugs, Dreams and the Making of China.* Sydney: Picador, 2011.
Ma, Min, and Ai Xiaofeng. *Zhang Jian and the World Exposition in the Early Years of the 20th Century: An Inter-Cultural Historical Observation.* Huazhong Normal University, China. http://www.princeton.edu/~collcutt/doc/MaMin_English.pdf, 4.
Miles, M. "Disability and Dialogue in East Asia: Social and Educational Responses from Ancient to Recent Times." Rev. ed. 4.0, August 2007. www.independentliving.org/docs7/miles2.
Outlook for the Blind 10 (Spring 1917) 4, editorial.
Paddle, Sarah. "To Save the Women of China from Fear, Opium and Bound Feet: Australian Women Missionaries in Early Twentieth-Century China." *Itinerario: International Journal on the History of European Expansion and Global Interaction* 34/3 (2010) 67–82.
Pollock, John C. *The Cambridge Seven.* Leicester, UK: IVP, 1966.
Preston, Diana. *The Boxer Rebellion: The Dramatic Story of China's War on Foreigners that Shook the World in the Summer of 1900.* New York: Berkley, 2001.

Reeson, Margaret. "Thomas Hassall." In *Australian Dictionary of Evangelical Biography (ADEB)*, 1:159–60. Melbourne: Melbourne University Press, 1960.

Reinders, Eric. *Borrowed Gods and Foreign Bodies: Christian Missionaries Imagine Chinese Religion*. Berkeley: University of California Press, 2004.

Roberts, Claire. *Photography in China*. London: Reaktion Books, 2013.

Schifrin, H. Z. *Sun Yat Sen and the Origins of the Chinese Revolution*. Center for Chinese Studies. Publications. Berkeley: University of California Press, 2010.

Stewart, J., and D. Hassall. *The Hassall Family: Celebrating 200 Years in Australia*. Hassall Family Bicentenary Association, 1998.

Stock, Eugene. *For Christ and Fuh-kien: The Story of the Fuh-kien Mission of the Church Missionary Society*. London: Church Missionary Society, 1904.

Tang, P. K. "Mission in China: A History of the Church Missionary Society," 1–3. In http://asiacms.net/wordpress/wp-content/uploads/.../.

Taylor, Hudson. *Dr and Mrs. Hudson Taylor and the China Inland Mission*. Vol. 2, *The Growth of a Work of God*. London: China Inland Mission, 1911.

Teale, R. "Hassall, Eliza Marsden (1834–1917)." In *The Australian Dictionary of Biography*: http://adb.anu.edu.au/biography/hassall-eliza-marsden-12970/text23439.

Walker, David. *Anxious Nation: Australia and the Rise of Asia 1850–1939*. Brisbane: University of Queensland Press, 1999.

Watson, Mary E. *Robert and Louisa Watson: In Life and Death*. London: Marshall, 1895.

Welch, Ian H. "Mary Reed of Australia and the China Inland Mission." Working paper. August 2014. https://openresearch-repository.anu.edu.au/bitstream/1885/13040/1/Welch%20Mary%20Reed%202014.pdf.

———. "Nellie, Topsy and Annie: Australian Anglican Martyrs, Project Canterbury," 2004. In http://anglicanhistory.org/asia/china/welch2004.pdf.

———. "The Vegetarians (Ys'ai hui): A Secret Society in Fujian, China, 1895." *Journal of the Oriental Society of Australia* 39–40/2 (2007–2008) 468–83.

White, W. C. "Three Weeks with Opium Smokers in a Chinese Village." *Chinese Recorder and Missionary Journal* 37 (1906) 628–31.

Wilkinson, Amy Oxley. "School for Blind Boys, Foochow, China." In *Report of the International Conference on the Blind and Exhibition of the Arts and Industries of the Blind*, 445–49. London: Westminster, 1914.

———. *Soul-Lighted School*. London: Church Missionary Society, n.d.

Wilkinson, George. Family Collection, Cadbury Library, University of Birmingham.

———. "Cases of Abdominal Surgery." *China Medical Journal* (January 1920) 1–.

———. "Loan of an Idol Temple." *Mercy and Truth* October (1909) 333–41. http://www.chinesemedalblog.com.

Wong. H. R. *And There Was Light*. Vol. 4. London: Forgotten Books, 1934.

Yarrington, W. H. H. *The Blind Chinese Boy*. New South Wales: Church Missionary Society, n.d..

Yarwood, Alenander T. "Samuel Marsden." In *The Australian Dictionary of Evangelical Biography (ADEB)*, edited by Brian Dickey, 250–53. Sydney: Evangelical Historical Association, 1994.